Making Waves

Making Waves

Fifty Stories about SHARING LOVE and CHANGING THE WORLD

Judy Clemens

Illustrations by
David Leonard

HERALD PRESS

Harrisonburg, Virginia

Herald Press
PO Box 866, Harrisonburg, Virginia 22803
www.HeraldPress.com

Library of Congress Cataloging-in-Publication Data
Names: Clemens, Judy, author. | Leonard, David, 1979- illustrator.
Title: Making waves : fifty stories about sharing love and changing the world /
    Judy Clemens ; illustrated by David Leonard.
Description: Harrisonburg, Virginia : Herald Press, 2020. | Audience: Ages 9-12 |
    Audience: Grades 4-6
Identifiers: LCCN 2020005982 (print) | LCCN 2020005983 (ebook) |
    ISBN 9781513806099 (paperback) | ISBN 9781513806112 (ebook)
Subjects: LCSH: Christian life—Anecdotes—Juvenile literature. | Christian
    biography—Juvenile literature.
Classification: LCC BV4517 .C584 2020 (print) | LCC BV4517 (ebook) |
    DDC 270.092/2—dc23
LC record available at https://lccn.loc.gov/2020005982
LC ebook record available at https://lccn.loc.gov/2020005983

Contents

Introduction

*J*esus said, "Blessed are the peacemakers."

But what does this mean? Who are the peacemakers? What are they doing?

The Bible tells us: "Love your enemies. Do good to those who hate you. Bless those who curse you. Pray for those who mistreat you" (Luke 6:27-28).

But is this the only way to make peace? No! The Bible tells us to work for peace in other ways as well:[1]

If you have two shirts, share one.

Sing of love and justice.

Feed the hungry, give water to the thirsty, and clothe the naked.

Visit the sick and those in prison.

Learn to work together.

---

1   See a list of related Bible verses on pages 212–14).

Care for the small.

Be creative! Use your gifts and abilities.

Don't seek revenge.

Respect others.

See goodness in everyone.

Train well and run hard for the finish line.

See God's power in our weakness.

Be responsible for the animals and the earth.

Never walk away from someone who needs help.

Turn your weapons into tools that bring life.

Welcome the immigrant.

Speak out.

Seek justice.

Love God, love self, love neighbor.

There are so many ways to work toward peace!

One thing to keep in mind—while peacemaking means working with others to make the world a better place, it does not mean that it's okay for people to harm you or others physically or emotionally. If you need help in that kind of situation, talk to a trusted adult. Peace is about respect and well-being for everyone, including the peacemaker!

The people featured in this book spread peace in many different ways. May you find something that sparks a passion for peace in you!

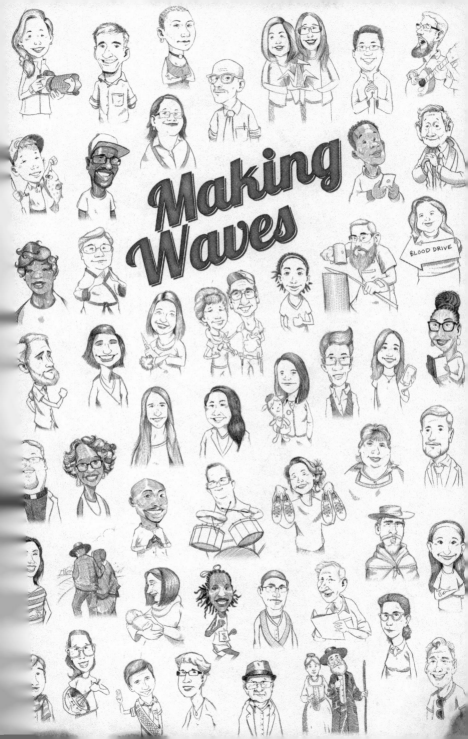

Katie Stagliano

Gardener

Who would ever dream that a tiny seedling from a third-grade classroom could turn into a forty-pound cabbage? And who would think that one cabbage plant could lead to a nonprofit organization that feeds thousands of people each year?

Nine-year-old Katie Stagliano brought a tiny cabbage plant home from school. She dutifully watered and cared for it in her backyard. Eventually it grew to a "freaky" size. Her family agreed—they could never eat it all themselves! Katie knew the cabbage was special. She donated it to Tricounty Family Ministries, a soup kitchen, where it would help feed 275 people.

When Katie got to the soup kitchen, she saw all the hungry people standing in line. She knew right then that she wanted to feed more people. She wanted to end hunger all around her country.

"I realized that the faces I saw were families just like mine who had fallen on hard times," she says. "I thought if my cabbage could help feed 275 people, then imagine how many people a garden could feed."

Katie went to the headmaster of Pinewood Preparatory School, the school she attended in South Carolina. She asked for permission to start a garden on the school grounds and to get her classmates to help plant it. He not only gave her permission—he gave her a plot of land the size of a football field!

Katie didn't want to stop there. Not only did she continue planting her own garden, but she made it possible for other kids to cultivate one too. Each year she accepts applications from nine- to sixteen-year-olds who want to plant a garden. Those accepted receive funding from donations for the cost of planting, gardening supplies, and help from a master gardener. Her nonprofit, called Katie's Krops, supports each garden in whatever way it can.

"We have gardens of all different sizes at churches, Boys and Girls Clubs, schools, backyards, community centers, and 4-H clubs," Katie says. "It's really incredible how the gardens continue growing year after year, and how they're passed down to other kids when someone goes to college."

As an incentive for the young gardeners, Katie held Katie's Krops camps every summer before she went to college. She invited ten of her gardeners to come to the WP Rawl Farm in South Carolina. There they learned new growing techniques that taught them "green" gardening methods. Did you know that ladybugs can be used to control aphids instead of using harmful chemicals? After camp, her gardeners knew all kinds of growing tricks like that!

Katie's Krops now supports over one hundred gardens in thirty-one states. They donate fresh produce to soup kitchens, emergency food programs, cancer centers, and directly to families in need. In 2018 they donated over 38,000 pounds of fresh food. Katie's very first garden still supplies fresh, garden-to-table monthly meals at Summerville Baptist Church. In one year they serve over 2,200 meals!

Katie knows there are over eight hundred million people who go hungry each day, all over the world. She doesn't have any plans to stop expanding her mission.

"My vision is to have five hundred gardens in all fifty states, and then I'd love to start Katie's Krops internationally," she says. "I know when you put all our growers together—no matter how large or small their efforts—we're making a huge impact."

Katie's Krops is doing what Katie set out to do all along— end hunger garden by garden.

Adi Walujo

Pastor on the lawn

One of the churches in the Javanese Mennonite Church sits in the middle of a rural area in Indonesia. Christians are a minority in this country. Most of the people in the region are Muslim.

One day the congregation had just finished celebrating Easter when a group of Muslims came into the yard and placed a piece of paper on the church door. They said the church would no longer be open, and the people could not go in. The people from the church were shocked. Many of them were related to the people who brought the paper. Why were they doing this?

Pastor Adi Walujo told the congregation they wouldn't stop worshiping. The church was not a building. It was the people who were the body of Christ. They continued meeting at the church on Sundays, but instead of going into the building, they met on the lawn. They even met there during the rainy season! They would use umbrellas and plastic tarps to cover their heads.

The congregation prayed for their Muslim friends and neighbors, asking God how they could talk with them. Pastor Walujo and others from his church went to the Muslim leaders and asked why they had closed the church. There was no clear answer. They were simply told that they lived in a Muslim area, so they should go somewhere else if they wanted to worship God in their way.

But Pastor Walujo and his congregation were surprised by what happened next.

On the church lawn there was a well that was used by the entire community. During the time the Mennonites were not allowed to go into their church, they still let their neighbors—most of them Muslim—use the fresh water. The people who used the water told the Muslim leaders that even though the Mennonites had been cut off from their church building, they had not kept anyone from getting the water they needed.

Eight months after the church was closed, one of the Muslim leaders came to Pastor Walujo. "Brother," he said, "you Christians are good people. We realize that you are a part of the community. Although we closed your church, the water from your well is still running around. It gives life to our people in the community." And then he said, "I apologize. We decided to allow you to use your church building again to worship your God."

Pastor Walujo and his congregation discovered that although being treated unfairly because of your faith is difficult, you can still live out what you believe. The Javanese Mennonite Church is a church that practices peace. So they chose to actively show love to their neighbors by praying for them and allowing them to use the well.

This experience helped the congregation grow in their love for God and others. They learned to depend on God. They believed and trusted God to transform the situation and make it possible for them to worship in their church building again. Once the Muslim leaders reopened the building, they even allowed the church to place a cross on the front to show it was a Christian church.

"Before, maybe people didn't know the meaning of love," Pastor Walujo says. "Maybe they couldn't see the impact of the love that we feel in our lives." Pastor Walujo believes he and his congregation had a special gift from God through this experience. "We grew, our faith grew, and our relationships with the Muslims grew."

Ashleigh Scully

Wildlife photographer

Ashleigh Scully has always had a passion for animals and wildlife. When she was eight years old, she traveled to Alaska with her grandparents and some of her cousins. She took along a simple camera and spent her vacation taking pictures of everything. The animals she photographed included bears, killer whales, sea lions, and bald eagles. After she got home, she wanted to continue photographing animals, and she's done just that.

Ashleigh has grown in her craft, winning awards and gaining recognition for her talent. While it's amazing and fun to have her work noticed by *National Geographic* and the National Audubon Society, what she really hopes is to be a voice for God's creation. "I want to help animals," she says. "I will never stop loving wildlife, and I want my photography to make a difference."

Ashleigh works hard to keep peace between humans and animals by helping people see personality in the images. "I try to present wildlife in a way that shares a story and makes the viewer care about the subject," she says. "I enjoy capturing wildlife in settings and situations that show emotion."

One of her goals is to have more opportunities to photograph endangered species. She likes taking "pretty pictures," but she really wants to capture images that are meaningful. At one point, Ashleigh spoke out against trophy hunting of grizzly bears in Wyoming. "As a young wildlife photographer," Ashleigh says, "I've been fortunate to observe a lot of bear behavior in the wild in both Wyoming and Alaska. It has been my hope that by sharing images of unique bear behavior and intimate family moments, it would inspire the younger generation to grow up with a greater respect for our country's wildlife." Ashleigh believes that grizzly bears deserve to live life as wild animals. They are not objects to collect, but a species worth celebrating and protecting.

Ashleigh published two books of photographs to raise money for animal conservation. The first was about red foxes. It raised over $3,000 for preserving open space in her town. The second book featured owls near her home. Proceeds went toward land for conservation and a raptor rehabilitation center.

Ashleigh also enjoys working with mentors and other photographers who have a passion for animals. It's good to get together with people who feel strongly about a common goal. "Wildlife photographers are all on the same team because they care about their subjects," she says.

Ashleigh continues to photograph wildlife in the hope that she will make a difference in the world of animal conservation. She would like others' respect for animals to grow into love for wildlife and a desire to see it protected. "I think a lot of animals are misunderstood," she says, "and seeing a photo of them in a beautiful setting may help people appreciate them more."

After a recent trip to photograph more grizzlies, she posted photos on social media. "I hope my photos will change people's minds about some species," she wrote. "I find that the power of an image has the ability to change others' perspectives. The connection that one can make with an image has the power to create change. I hope that through my images of these bears, any negatives you all can think of will disappear, and you will see the side of bears that I saw. The side where bears show countless emotions through protecting and loving their families, just as we all do for ours."

Anderson Sa

AfroReggae musician

Anderson Sa grew up in Vigário Geral, one of Brazil's most violent slums. This area, known as a "favela" in Brazil, was filled with violence, poverty, and drugs. When Anderson was young, he looked forward to the day when he could join a gang and be a part of that life. As soon as he turned thirteen, he began working for the Red Command, the most powerful gang in the area. He helped with the sale of drugs and weapons, and attacked other favelas and dealers. But his circle of friends began to grow smaller. The other boys and men he knew were being killed, disappearing, or getting arrested because of their work with the gangs. Life was difficult, and the stress of losing friends to violence was becoming too much for him.

In 1993, when Anderson was a teenager, the police raided Vigário Geral and killed twenty-one people, including Anderson's brother. Anderson decided he was ready to move out of gang life and find a way to make his community a better place.

"I started to ask why we wanted to kill each other," Anderson said. "How do I end the violence? Can I use music as an instrument of change?"

Along with his friend José Junior, Anderson cofounded an organization called the AfroReggae Cultural Group. Their mission is to offer the arts to youth, to give them an alternative to a life of drugs and other illegal activities. In the hope of reducing disease, crime, and the use of drugs, they introduce local teens to art, music, and dance. In one year alone, they offered training and workshops to over two thousand youth in over sixty programs. Their goal is to bring hope and peace to their communities through culture.

It was difficult to start a program in gang territory. So AfroReggae made a compromise with the local gangs in order to safely operate. They promised not to interfere with the gang activity but to work on their own projects to reduce crime. This was the only way they could operate within the gang's territory and build community around the arts.

Besides classes, AfroReggae offers job training and employment to formerly convicted young people to help give them a second chance. They work to build the self-esteem of young people, and also to help them learn about health, AIDS awareness, human rights, and education. They train them to work in service and entertainment businesses. AfroReggae is also trying to change how criminals and the police see one another, in the hope of building better relationships between them. Besides the organization in Brazil, the AfroReggae Cultural Group has chapters in Colombia and England.

The organization raises money for their programs by giving concerts and selling albums. Besides their main bands, they also have two bands that feature young musicians—Afro Lata, made up of ten- to fifteen-year-olds, and Afro Samba, which includes seven- to twelve-year-olds.

The work that AfroReggae does with these youth is helping to give them options other than violence and crime, but Anderson realizes there is still a lot of work to be done. He tries to be positive. "For every kid our movement attracts to percussion class there are five waiting to join the drug army," he says. "We are happy to have that one kid."

Olivea Borden

Dollmaker

O livea Borden was attending her Colorado high school when she made a doll in art class using recycled materials. Her teacher loved the doll so much he bought it for his daughter! Soon after, Olivea and her family went on a mission trip to Nicaragua. She saw how girls there lived in poverty. They didn't have any dolls or other items to play with. "Most families in Nicaragua are living on two dollars a day or less," she says; "thus buying a toy is rarely a priority." Money is needed for the basics of food and shelter.

This bothered Olivea. She knew how important toys were, both for joy and for children's development. She wanted to make sure the girls in that Nicaraguan village had toys too. So Olivea began making dolls and selling them locally. With the money she earned, she was able to make more dolls, and soon had more orders than she could fill! Her motto was "Buy a doll, give a doll," because with the money she earned from selling a doll she was able to send another doll to a girl in Nicaragua. "The gift of a doll communicates to these children that they are loved," she says. Olivea wants to remind these children that they have value and have been created for a purpose.

Olivea won a contest for young business owners and used her prize money to hire a woman who needed a job. That got her thinking. If she could hire someone in her community to make dolls, why couldn't she hire people in Nicaragua too? She went back to Nicaragua and taught some of the women how to make the dolls. The women who graduated from "Dolly Academy" were all given a diploma and the opportunity for employment. "You should have seen their faces!" says Olivea. Her new motto became "Buy a doll, give a doll, give a woman a job."

A local Colorado retailer agreed to sell the dolls. The women who make them are given fair wages, which means money not only for making the dolls, but for materials as well. The women are making enough to support their families—much more than two dollars a day!

Olivea's business, called Oli-Bo-Bolly, has grown so much that there are now dolls on every continent but Antarctica. Each doll comes with a message translated into the recipient's native language, whether English, Spanish, or another language:

You are beautiful / Tu eres hermosa

You are one of a kind / Tu eres unica

You are loved / Tu eres amada

You are special / Tu eres especial

You are created for a purpose / Tu eres creado para une preposito

The idea for the dolls first came from learning about how much is thrown away in the United States. The dolls are all made from leftover material, which adds another lifesaving aspect to Olivea's mission. "In my sophomore science class, I learned that 85 percent of textiles in our landfills are still wearable," she says. "That hit me hard. Why make new materials to use when we have these? I want to help decrease the expansion of landfills to perhaps give us a bit more time to enjoy the world we've been given."

Olivea feels so grateful that she not only helps girls feel loved, but has been able to offer women tools to help themselves. "I think we each have our own little part to play," she says. "It's important to help people feel God's love. You never know when it's going to change their life."

Tyler Clark

Drummer

*T*yler Clark showed an interest in drums when he was quite young. He enjoyed playing a toy drum whenever he could. Fast-forward to his fourteenth birthday, when his family surprised him with a full set of acoustic drums! He spent hours and hours every week playing on his drum set. He never took lessons. Instead, he trained by ear and practice; now he joins a worship team at church, leading a room filled with praise and singing. This amazes his mother. She understands he has limitations in some areas of his life. But she sees that he has a natural God-given gift to hear music, single out the drumming part, and play really well.

You see, Tyler is a unique person. He's a man living with Down syndrome. Down syndrome is the name of a condition where someone is born with an extra chromosome. Chromosomes are part of our DNA, which make up who we are. If someone has Down syndrome, it means their brain and body will work a bit differently than someone born without it.

"If Tyler didn't have Down syndrome, he honestly would just be another young adult doing his thing at church," his mom, Karmen, says. "But because God gave Tyler a unique and special genetic makeup, he plays a much different role. He is noticed. Tyler doesn't hide who he is. He is very sensitive and caring of others, asking folks how they are doing, reminding others often about wonderful and meaningful experiences he had with them in the past. Tyler is a lover. He asks for hugs at church from many as he meets up with them. He ends conversations with friends at church with an 'I love you.' How often, even at church, do we hear a fellow brother or sister say out loud that they love us? Many choose to bless Tyler back by saying, 'I love you, too, Tyler.' What a good way to show God's love and bring unity amongst people."

Tyler is also hilarious, and loves to have fun. He doesn't hold back or worry what other people think. God has given him the ability to live fully as a child of God. He brings happiness and joy, silliness, and excitement when he engages others at church. Tyler is more than just the drummer at Clinton Frame Mennonite Church. He is a valued member of the community not only for the gifts he brings, but for the person he is.

"You see, the natural thing we might think when we hear 'Down syndrome,' is that he might be missing something," his mom says. "We picture limitations, we see physical impairments. But God has chosen to take Tyler's label

of Down syndrome, and all the negative and limiting con-
notations that are typically associated with it, and throw it
all out the window. Instead, God has given Tyler extraordinary talents and abilities. He's given Tyler the ability to
consistently remind people they are loved and cared about.
God does this without hesitation."

"I have learned so much over the years from being Tyler's
mom," Karmen says. "I have been humbled over and over
as I watch him live out what God would intend for us all.
That ability to love everyone, without hesitation, without
judgment, and find so much happiness and joy in doing so."

Emma González

Gun control activist

On February 14, 2018, a shooter entered Marjory Stoneman Douglas (MSD) High School in Parkland, Florida, and killed seventeen people, injuring many others. After that awful day, many of the students felt that it was important to work for gun control to help protect schools. One of those students was Emma González.

Emma, a senior at Marjory Stoneman Douglas, worked with several other students to organize a demonstration called March for Our Lives to make people aware of what happened at their school. They wanted to make people think about what needs to be done to stop gun violence in the United States. This protest took place in Washington, D.C., in March, a month after the shooting. On the same day, hundreds of thousands of students participated in marches throughout the country, and even around the world. Students walked out of their classes to show their solidarity with the Parkland students.

Emma gave a speech at the demonstration in Washington, D.C., rallying others to work for new gun laws and regulations. She spoke for two minutes and then became quiet. She wanted people to think about the amount of time it took the shooter to kill seventeen people. While the crowd chanted "Never again!" and yelled her name, Emma stood silently on the stage, tears streaming down her face. Finally, she spoke again.

"Since the time that I came out here, it has been six minutes and twenty seconds," she said. "The shooter has ceased shooting and will soon abandon his rifle, blend in with the students as they escape, and walk free for an hour before arrest. Fight for your lives before it's someone else's job."

Emma's speech was heard by millions of people, and she has become one of the faces and voices of the fight for school safety and gun control. She helped create the Never Again MSD movement, also known by the hashtag #NeverAgain. She speaks with state legislators and other lawmakers. She has been on television many times, including *The Ellen DeGeneres Show* and a CNN town hall that aired all over the world. When she joined Twitter, she gained a million followers in less than ten days. She believes everyone should be involved in trying to end gun violence.

"In a little over six minutes, seventeen of our friends were taken from us, fifteen more were injured, and everyone—absolutely everyone in the Douglas community—was forever altered," Emma said in her speech at the march in Washington, D.C. "Everyone who was there understands.

Everyone who has been touched by the cold grip of gun violence understands."

The work of Emma and her fellow students has gotten positive results. In March 2019, Florida passed the Marjory Stoneman Douglas High School Safety Act. It says that people must be at least twenty-one years old to buy a gun, establishes waiting periods and background checks before people can make a gun purchase, and makes it illegal to sell guns to people who have been arrested for violent crimes. The governor of Florida signed the bill and said, "To the students of Marjory Stoneman Douglas High School, you made your voices heard. You didn't let up and you fought until there was change."

Emma will keep fighting for change by continuing her education. She is now a student at the New College of Florida, in Sarasota.

Erek Hansen

Recycler

When Erek Hansen was nine years old he saw an ad in *National Geographic Kids* magazine. The ad asked people to send in jeans to help set a Guinness World Record for the largest collection of clothing recycled. The jeans would be shredded into cotton fibers and turned into housing insulation to help people in disaster areas. Erek started to think.

What if he organized a denim drive? Could he encourage people in his town to bring their old jeans? Then something people usually throw away could be turned into something to help others. He learned that approximately five hundred pairs of old jeans could be recycled to insulate an entire home. That sounded great to him.

Erek's first denim drive was held in the driveway at his house. He collected a thousand pairs of jeans from friends and neighbors, as well as from members of his church and local community. An employee at a local alternative energy company heard about the project and held a separate drive, which collected six hundred items. Altogether, Erek sent 1,684 pieces of denim to the national headquarters of National Geographic. Enough to insulate three houses!

After this first denim drive, Erek decided he wanted to keep going. He loved knowing that not only was he keeping all those jeans out of landfills, but they were being put to good use. With the help of his family, he formed an organization called EcoErek, and partnered with a recycling nonprofit. He continued coordinating denim collections. The material he received was shipped to Blue Jeans Go Green, an organization that recycles denim. Besides holding annual denim drives, he also set up drop boxes around northwest Ohio. Through Habitat for Humanity, the jeans have gone on to help many people affected by natural disasters, such as those whose homes were destroyed by Hurricane Katrina on the Gulf Coast or Hurricane Sandy on the East Coast.

Eventually, Erek also began collecting shoes. Shoes in good shape were directed to people who could use them. Shoes that had reached the end of their usefulness were recycled into items such as carpet padding, playground mulch, and athletic surfaces. At last count Erek's organization had collected over 33,000 pieces of denim and 20,000 pairs of shoes.

When Erek was preparing to go to college, he realized he might not be able to do as much work with his recycling initiative. He changed the name from EcoErek to Go Green Ohio so his name wouldn't be attached and so others could more easily do the work when he couldn't. He didn't want the work to stop just because he had to focus on school-work. Because of his preparation, Erek's dream of making a difference through recycling continues, even while he's at college. A fifth-grade student from his home school district stepped up to take some of the workload, and they work together.

Erek encourages other young people to "dream big" when it comes to finding ways to help people and take care of the earth. "My dream started out really small with the denim drive at my house," he says. "I never thought it would get this big." Erek's work not only helps in his region, but has inspired others to recycle. He encourages everyone to get out and do their part. "The more good in the world," he says, "the better!"

Lauren Cunningham
Blood drive recruiter

I want to make blood drives happen in order to help kids like me," Lauren Cunningham says. Who are kids like her? Well, Lauren describes them as her "Cancer Friends."

When Lauren was nine, she was diagnosed with leukemia. After experiencing some scary symptoms, such as dizziness, droopiness in her face, and terrible headaches, she had to stay in the hospital for weeks before she was stabilized. Then she began treatments, which meant feeling sick and tired, losing her hair, and missing out on things her friends were doing. Lauren still has to deal with physical aftereffects from chemotherapy and radiation, but she's in remission, which means that, at the moment, Lauren is cancer free.

The experience was difficult and exhausting, so Lauren goes all out to make things better for her peers. One of Lauren's main goals is to make sure other children like her receive all the blood they need. During Lauren's illness she had over eighty blood transfusions. Eighty! She remembers how it felt to have the new blood coursing through her system. "Before I would get transfusions, I would feel tired," she says, "and by the end of the transfusion I would feel energized and ready to go shopping!"

When Lauren was first diagnosed, people from her mom's work formed a group called Team Lauren and organized a blood drive, which was held at Lauren's church. They created T-shirts and held fundraisers to get the word out about donating. Now, even though Lauren doesn't need blood transfusions anymore, she knows there are many children who do. Team Lauren continues, under Lauren's care.

"Lauren's main job for the blood drives," her mother says, "is as a recruiter. She's not shy about getting people to donate. She asks friends, bugs her teachers, and hands out Red Cross flyers. She sends out postcards asking people to donate, then follows up with thank you cards. Local businesses will hang signs and donate food or gift cards to those who give. One time a local radio station contacted her, and she talked on air. She does whatever she can to get the word out. Then, on the day of the drive, she'll attend, handing out 'Thank you for being a lifesaver' notes. She wants to show the donors a real person who needed blood, and how beneficial it is."

But Lauren doesn't just work for blood drives. She does everything she can to brighten the days of kids dealing with cancer and to let them know they're not forgotten. Lauren's school district is very supportive of her efforts.

One September, which is Childhood Cancer Awareness Month, Lauren planned a day for everyone to wear yellow. Students stood on the football field in the pattern of a cancer ribbon, and a drone took their picture. Lauren sent this to her Cancer Friends to let them know Bath school was thinking of them. Other groups, such as the fire department or school choirs, also participate in special events and take pictures, which Lauren sends to kids who need support. That way they know they're not alone—even if it feels like it—in their hospital rooms.

Lauren's illness was frightening and difficult. Instead of feeling sorry for herself, Lauren chooses to make things better for others. She takes to heart a verse from Matthew 25—"I was sick and you took care of me." Lauren can't take away the suffering of her Cancer Friends, but she can do a lot to ease the way. Go, Team Lauren!

Safari Mutabesha

Refugee preacher

*P*astor Safari Mutabesha comes from a people called the Banyamulenge. They are cattle herders who live in the Democratic Republic of the Congo. Over the years they have had to move many times to find green pastures for their animals. A famine finally forced them high into the mountains, where they now live. Over the past twenty years there's been a lot of conflict among their country's leaders, and the Banyamulenge have been mistreated because of their ethnic background. They are unloved and unwanted, and many of them have been killed simply because of who they are.

Safari was the choir leader at the church where his father was the pastor. He loved training young people to sing. But one day Safari had a dream in which God told him, "Your time in this church is over." So Safari walked to the next town, where he found a Mennonite church. He knew this was where he was supposed to be.

The Mennonites taught Safari about the importance of forgiveness and about working for peace and reconciliation—repairing relationships that have been broken. But even though Safari knew this was where his ministry was leading him, life was still difficult because he was Banyamulenge.

After some time, Safari learned that his parents had been killed while fleeing their home. Safari was frightened, and decided it was time for him to leave as well. He fled to Burundi and lived in a refugee camp there for three years before returning to Congo. But it was still too dangerous to live in Congo, so he left again. This time he fled to a refugee camp in Malawi.

The camp in Malawi was filled with hopelessness and despair. People did not get along, and there was anger and division. Safari decided to start his own church in the camp. He and a few friends went from tent to tent, speaking about the love of Jesus and offering hope and compassion. "I often shared from Ezekiel," he says, "where the prophet talks about how God had driven his people from their land and dispersed them among the nations because they had forsaken him. But God also would offer forgiveness: 'A new heart I will give you, and a new spirit I will put within you; and I will remove from your body the heart of stone and give you a heart of flesh' [Ezekiel 36:26 NRSV]."

Their new church grew. They focused on loving and forgiving their enemies. They shared a simple message: Because God loves us, we must love each other.

Another man from Congo came to the refugee camp, and Pastor Safari welcomed him into his home. The man joined the church and became part of the congregation. After a while Safari learned that this very man killed Safari's parents. Safari realized that his belief in the teachings of Jesus was being put to the test. If Safari preached to others that they must love and forgive, then he must do it also! With God's help, and the help of his church, Safari was able to forgive the man for what he had done to Safari's family.

Safari continues to preach God's message of love and reconciliation. There are now eleven churches in the area where he lives. The churches are built on the peace and for- giveness of Christ.

Pastor Safari loves what God is doing in these congre- gations, and it gives his heart much joy to see the churches thriving. He says, "To God be the glory!"

Kris Polega

Tae kwon do instructor

As a peacemaker seeking to prevent violence and transform conflict, I pledge to:

Have esteem for myself and respect for others.

Set my heart to courage and my mind to wisdom.

Be responsible for my emotions and actions.

Act with honor, compassion, and self-control.

Use my head rather than my hands in conflict.

Seek to do no harm to others or myself, and

resolve problems in positive ways for peace.

Students at Peacemakers Academy begin each training session by reciting this pledge. It is a promise they make when they join the school. The academy asks the students to honor the pledge as much as possible in their lives.

Kris Polega became a student at Peacemakers when she saw that her children, also students at the academy, weren't being taught "how to fight," but rather how to protect themselves. They were learning to find inner peace and harmony, how to be respectful toward others, and how to "do conflict well." Kris began teaching at Peacemakers when her instructor asked her to help teach an afterschool program. At first she was nervous and scared, but she found she liked teaching. The program was a natural fit with her Church of the Brethren faith.

Kris graduated from seminary, which is school where people learn about the Bible and church leadership. Rather than becoming a traditional pastor, she serves in various roles within the church. She preaches once in a while, but her main job is teaching at the academy. She finds this to be a good way to serve God and teach peace.

Martial arts aren't the first thing people think of when they hear the word *peace*. But Kris says that tae kwon do isn't like what you see in the movies. Martial arts focuses on basic lessons like honor, integrity, compassion, perseverance, self-control, and respect—all things that lead to peace and handling conflict well. Basically, taking care of yourself leads to taking care of other people. Steve Thomas, who started Peacemakers, says that "hurt people hurt people." This means that people who feel bad about themselves often have problems knowing how to treat others.

Much of the Peacemakers program is about helping people feel more confident. "This was part of my own personal experience!" Kris says. "As a person wanting to go into ministry, but as a short woman, I was always afraid of larger, overbearing people. As I trained, I became more confident in my abilities to defend myself, which meant I could do ministry with people I would have been scared to even talk to before. Peacemakers also taught me how to talk with confidence in conflict, not as a means of 'winning' an argument, but as a way of radiating a calm, positive energy."

Another part of tae kwon do is community service. Students have a chance to interact with people and do things that may be a bit outside their comfort zone. This will hopefully help make them more understanding and respectful of others. Kris has been working to include more community service in her lessons.

When it all comes together, Peacemakers Academy teaches about peacemaking through respect for self and respect for others in every situation. Kris says, "When a person feels respected, they're more likely to be willing to work through conflict in a healthier manner. Obviously, we strive to respect everyone, but we understand it's hard to feel respect for everyone. We want our students to strive to show respect for all people."

Stanimir Katanic
Conscientious objector

The former Yugoslavia, like many countries, required all young men to serve in the military. Stanimir Katanic grew up in the Nazarene Church, which is part of the Anabaptist group of churches. Anabaptists believe in nonviolence. They do not join the armed forces. So when Stanimir turned twenty and he had to show up to serve, he knew what would happen. He would go to prison.

Stanimir stood before a panel of military leaders. He told them he would work and do whatever jobs were assigned to him. "But," he told them, "I will not compromise my faith. I will swear no oath of allegiance to an earthly government, and I refuse to use a weapon to kill another person." He would answer only to God. He would not do what his country wanted if it meant going against what Jesus taught.

The officers immediately handcuffed Stanimir and marched him to prison. He was placed in a room with two hundred violent criminals. He was given a gray jumpsuit to wear, and his name was replaced with a number. For the next four years he was called simply 2032B.

The ward where Stanimir lived did not have enough cots, and he had to sleep on the floor. During the day he worked in the shop. Because he kept quiet and did his work, he was not beaten as often as the other prisoners. He was hungry most of the time. When he did get bread, it was often stolen by the other prisoners. Breakfast and supper were spooned into a bowl he carried with him at all times.

Stanimir was very lonely. There were other Nazarene young men at the prison, but the guards kept them separated so they couldn't talk. His family tried to send him food and letters, but most of the time the guards would not give them to him. Stanimir was not even allowed to have a Bible.

Finally, after four years, Stanimir was released from prison. He went home and married Kata, his childhood sweetheart. After several months Kata became pregnant. Stanimir was going to be a father! But then he got a letter. It said he had to come back to the courthouse.

When Stanimir arrived at court, the judge asked him if he was now ready to serve in the military. Stanimir didn't understand. He had done his time in prison. The judge didn't care. When Stanimir said he still could not pledge his allegiance to Yugoslavia or kill another person, the judge sent him to prison again. Stanimir was not allowed to say goodbye to his wife and family. He trusted that his relatives would take care of Kata and their baby.

Stanimir was sentenced to four and a half years in a gray, dreary prison. The temperature was often either extremely hot or extremely cold. He worked long days of hard labor. Then one day, when he had been there for three and a half years, he was released. He was so grateful to go home to Kata and their son, Miroslav.

The years away from his family were very difficult and harsh. But Stanimir would not change what he did. He believes he did the right thing. He would not kill anyone, and he would not swear his allegiance to Yugoslavia or any other country. His allegiance is to God.

"I never look for shortcuts in my faith," he says, "and neither should you."

Isabelle and Katherine Adams

Origami sisters

When Isabelle and Katherine Adams were little girls, they learned some troubling facts. Millions of people in the world, many of them children, do not have access to clean drinking water. Of those children, many are unable to go to school because they need to spend most of their time walking to get what water is available. Some must walk seven miles each way to find water! Katherine and Isabelle also learned that contaminated—or polluted— drinking water makes people sick, and that every twenty seconds a child dies from a waterborne illness.

Isabelle and Katherine wanted to do something about this crisis. They decided to make handcrafted origami ornaments that they would exchange for donations. Those donations would go to build a well in an Ethiopian community. Their parents helped them start their organization, which they called Paper for Water.

The goal for their first project was to raise $500. When they were finished, they had over $10,000, fully funding the $9,200 well in Ethiopia. Most wells cost between $10,000 and $20,000. Their community and church rallied around them to make this happen.

The sisters' desire to help people continued after their first fundraiser. They planned more projects and continued making origami. Katherine and Isabelle also wanted to get others involved. People in their Texas town and across the country may not have needed wells for clean water, but they were "thirsty" in other ways. They wanted to do something meaningful.

Volunteers do all sorts of things for the organization. Some fold paper, some teach others how to do the origami, and others take care of public relations. If someone comes along who is good at something and wants to help, the organization finds a way to use that person's talents. Through Paper for Water, hundreds of people have discovered that when they are helping someone else, it makes a difference in their own life and the lives of others.

Paper for Water gives the money they raise to a drilling company called Living Water International for projects in developing countries, and to Dig Deep for projects in the United States. Through the work of Living Water International, Paper for Water has supplied wells to orphanages, schools, and communities. They have raised over $1.6 million and have projects in twenty countries! Over

190 wells worldwide have been built with help from Paper for Water. The Adams sisters, now including their little sister, Trinity, are grateful that children can have clean water all day while they are at school. Thousands of kids are getting an education instead of trekking miles and miles every day just to get water.

Paper for Water doesn't just build wells and hope for the best. They also have partners who engage the communities in education around issues of hygiene and sanitation. This education helps the community develop a sense of ownership of the well, and equips them to sustain it so they have clean water for years to come.

Jesus is the living water. Paper for Water wants to serve others with joy and compassion. They invite everyone to join them in their desire and mission to provide clean water for all.

> But whoever drinks from the water that I will give will never be thirsty again. The water that I give will become in those who drink it a spring of water that bubbles up into eternal life. **—JOHN 4:14**

Dan West

Relief worker

"There has to be a better way to feed people," Dan West thought. He was working with the Church of the Brethren as the director of a relief program in Spain during the Spanish Civil War in the 1930s. Their organization had limited amounts of food to hand out, and Dan grew tired of seeing hungry people. How could a person live when they had only one cup of milk to drink?

The Church of the Brethren is a peace-loving denomination. Members strive to live a simple life of service. They want to make change in the world that will lead to peace and well-being for everyone. All people, according to the Brethren, have value in the eyes of God. Dan took this teaching to heart. He was a young husband and father when he left for his work in Spain. He struggled with seeing hungry families every day.

While serving there with a team of workers from the Church of the Brethren, Mennonites, and Quakers, Dan was required to drink a quart of milk a day and eat his entire ration of food. All workers were told to do this because otherwise they would be tempted to give their own food to hungry people, and they would lose their strength. Yet it was difficult for Dan to eat his portion because he knew how many others didn't have enough.

Every day, Dan saw the same people waiting for food. He couldn't imagine how it felt for them to not know where their food would come from each day. It had to be awful to feel that you couldn't take care of yourself and your family. He started to wonder, what if? What if instead of giving people a cup of milk, they gave them a whole cow? That way the people would have milk every day—enough for a whole family, maybe even a whole community. Would this work? Could Dan make this happen?

Dan went home to Indiana with his idea. He asked his friends and neighbors how this could be done.

"Have Faith," one farmer said.

"I'm trying," Dan said. "But I need your help."

"No," his friend said. "I mean have Faith, my Guernsey calf. She can be your first one."

Once the giving began, others offered more! Some volunteered to feed the calf, others to care for her. Two more people donated heifers. They were named Hope and Charity. With the help of neighbors and congregations, Dan found many people willing to donate young heifers, time, and money to families in need. The idea continued to grow, and Dan founded an organization now called Heifer International. Their motto? "Not a cup of milk, but a cow."

Today, the nonprofit is an international charity. They don't just give cows anymore. People all over the world also benefit from ownership of water buffalos, rabbits, goats, chickens, even honeybees! Heifer not only supplies animals to people, but also teaches them how to take care of them. Recipients of animals from Heifer also agree they will "pass on the gift" by giving eggs, milk, wool, or any baby animals to help others. This not only aids another family and community, but allows the first person to become a donor and help someone else.

Millions of people have been given a chance to thrive through this organization. One man had the vision. And Faith helped get it started.

Natalie Hampton

App designer

*L*ike many young people, perhaps even you, Natalie Hampton had some difficult years in middle and high school. She started out attending an all-girls academy, where she was bullied by other students. She received threatening emails, was pushed into lockers, and was told to her face that she was ugly and worthless. She ate lunch alone every day, watching as others enjoyed friendships and fun. One day she was physically attacked and went home with bleeding scratches on her face. Another time a girl threatened her with scissors, and no one stepped in to help. She tried to get other students and the teachers at her school to stop the bullying, but they said it was her fault, not the bullies'.

Natalie decided she wouldn't put up with it anymore. She transferred to another school, and on her first day another student came up to her in the hallway to ask if she needed help finding her classroom. In that moment, she felt seen and valued. That moment changed her life. At her old school, no one would say anything to help her, even when she was in danger, but at her new school, one small act of kindness made all the difference in how she felt about herself and the world around her. She was so glad she had found the strength, with the help of her parents and others around her, to do what was necessary to find a place of peace.

Natalie was happy in her new school, but she noticed that she also felt sad. She was sad that she was given a second chance while so many others were still dealing with bullies and loneliness. She realized if she didn't speak up and help those who were hurting, nothing would ever change. One simple way to show care for others was to invite them to sit with her at lunch. Whenever she saw someone sitting alone, or looking for a place to eat, she made them feel welcome at her table.

This new, simple plan was so successful that Natalie wanted to share it with people at other schools. She created a free and easy-to-use app called Sit With Us, which helps students find safe and welcoming groups to eat with. The motto is "When no one will sit with you, sit with us." People can also use the app to volunteer as a Sit With Us ambassador, pledging to welcome people and allow others to feel seen. Natalie believes that while adults can do their part to change a bullying environment, student-led projects are much more effective.

"All it takes is one person to change the world," Natalie says. "That person—starting right now—is you. It's up to you to make a difference in your communities, to leave this world better than the way you found it. A simple act of kindness can save a life."

The Sit With Us app went viral. It is now used by hundreds of thousands of people in at least eight different countries. Natalie travels to schools and conferences to spread the word about kindness and inclusiveness. She wants others to see they can be the difference, and that by working together, students can unite and make the world a better place, one lunch period at a time.

Dirk Willems

Anabaptist martyr

*I*n the mid-1500s a group of Christians called Anabaptists, or "re-baptizers," lived in Europe. They believed a person should be old enough to choose the way of Christ in order to be baptized, instead of being baptized as a baby. Today there are several Christian groups which are a part of the Anabaptist church. They include Mennonites, the Church of the Brethren, the Amish, and others.

In the sixteenth century, baptizing adults went against the rules of the Catholic and Protestant churches, which baptized babies as a part of their beliefs and religious rituals. The leaders of the larger churches created laws that made it illegal to be baptized again as an adult, or even to preach about this idea. Anabaptists who were caught were arrested, tried in court, and often killed for their beliefs.

One of these Anabaptists was named Dirk Willems. Dirk was born in the Netherlands in a town called Asperen. The authorities found and arrested him. He was held in the

Asperen castle, which had been turned into a prison. He was charged with being re-baptized, holding secret church services in his home, and allowing other people to be re-baptized at those services.

One winter night, knowing he faced execution if he stayed in prison, he made a rope out of knotted rags. He draped the rope out his window and escaped over the wall of the castle. Because he was thin from his imprisonment and not getting enough to eat, he had no trouble making his way over the barely frozen pond, called the Hondegat, which lay in front of the prison. A guard saw him escape and chased after him. Because the guard was well fed and larger than Dirk, he broke through the ice.

As Dirk ran away, he heard the crack of the ice and saw the guard plunge into the freezing water. The guard shouted for help, but no one else was there to come to his rescue. Dirk knew if he went back to save the man he would be re-captured and thrown once again into prison, but his belief in God and what Jesus would have done meant Dirk could not leave the man to drown. He stopped running, turned back, and pulled the guard from the water.

The guard, knowing that Dirk saved his life, wanted to let him go. But the chief magistrate was watching and told him he must remember his oath as a thief-catcher and officer of the peace. Dirk was too weak to run away again. The guard rearrested Dirk, and he was thrown back into prison. This time he was kept in a room at the top of a church tower, above the bell. The cell was heavily barred, and he was kept captive there until he was executed. Even at the end he was faithful to God and firm in his beliefs.

Dirk Willems showed love to his enemy, even when he knew he was risking his own life to do it. He realized that saving himself meant nothing if it would mean the guard would die while he escaped. Dirk chose love and compassion over hatred and fear.

The town of Asperen, where Dirk was born, put up a statue in his honor. They also have a street named after him. They want to remember his example and honor his decision to save the guard, even though it meant he himself would die.

Carol Roth

Reconciler

When Carol Roth was born, it was the middle of winter. She and her twin sister went to live with the Goods, a local Mennonite missionary couple, because their own parents were struggling to take care of them. Carol and her sister had been born very small, and their parents had three other little children. After the winter ended, Carol and her sister stayed in the home of the missionaries, with the understanding that the girls would be very involved in the lives of their Native American relatives. They would attend weddings, funerals, and other important events. Carol and her sister grew up in both cultures, learning about them and feeling at home.

"When I was young, I thought everyone grew up this way," Carol says of her bicultural youth. "As an adult, I think it has been good for me. I've learned the Anabaptist way of doing things as well as the Choctaw way of doing things."

When Carol got older and was married, she and her husband moved to Canada. After a while, she began to feel God calling her to return to her people, the Choctaw. Her husband agreed. They moved back to Mississippi. Carol felt that with her special upbringing she wanted to use those gifts to help build healthy relationships between the Choctaw and the Mennonites.

For a while, Carol served the Mississippi Band of Choctaw Indians as a tribal court administrator. She believed she was called to serve God with her gifts for leadership and organization, and to minister among Native American people. Unlike the dramatic ways that some in the Bible were called, "there was no lightning, but sensing the leading of the Lord through friends and in conversations with others," she says.

Carol also worked as a staff leader for Native Mennonite Ministries. "My passions and visions for the church are in the area of racial reconciliation," she says. Racial reconciliation means bringing people of different races together to listen to one another, finding justice for harm that has been done, and building new and healthy relationships. In her roles, Carol worked to share her knowledge and learn from others. She helped Native American churches to connect with one another, and to the Mennonite church.

Carol knows that different cultures don't always understand each other. Growing up both Choctaw and Mennonite, she saw a lot of things one group would do that the other would not be able to understand.

"For example," she says, "for Mennonites, hospitality tends to mean cooking special foods, setting the table with your best table linens and dishes, and making things especially nice when people come to eat with you. For Native Americans, the sharing of food is about the friendship, not the proper etiquette." Therefore, Native Americans generally serve what they have, and take time to visit with their guests. "These kinds of cultural differences can easily create misunderstandings, so I try to educate each culture about the other."

Carol learned many things from both parts of her life. With her work of racial reconciliation, she hopes to teach both groups of people about each other. "With Christian faith, I learned about connecting with God, the Creator, who is good," she says. And from her Choctaw people, "I learned that everything is sacred, and a lesson can be found in all things and experiences. I learned to love what is around me, even the small things, to respect everything, and to honor all."

Rev. Ken Heintzelman
Sanctuary pastor

W e are not the ones blessing the people," Rev. Ken Heintzelman says. "They are the ones blessing us." The immigrants, he means. They are a blessing.

Pastor Ken's congregation, the Shadow Rock United Church of Christ, is in Phoenix, Arizona, which is close to the southern border of the United States. The church is in an important spot to help immigrants trying to enter the United States. There are many different reasons immigrants might need their help.

Some immigrants are seeking asylum, which means they need to leave their own country because they're not safe there. They walk through dangerous land just to get to the United States. Sometimes they are accepted into the United States; sometimes they are not.

Other immigrants are already in the United States, but because they have been unable to get the right paperwork, the government wants to deport them, which means sending them back to their former homeland.

The people of Shadow Rock feel God's call to help these people through their hospitality ministry. Five years ago they began offering sanctuary—meaning a safe place for people in danger of being sent back to their former homeland. Shadow Rock let these people live at their church to give them time to work on ways they can remain in the country. Over the last four and a half years, Shadow Rock has provided sanctuary to seven adults. Two of them are still there, and one is a mother with seven children!

Today things are more difficult, and immigrants are no longer allowed to work their jobs or live with their families while waiting to find out if they can stay in the United States. This is why Shadow Rock provides housing to these people.

Shadow Rock also used to provide shelter for people who are asking for asylum. The people came to the border and filled out papers with the government explaining why they needed to come to the United States to be safe. The government would make a decision about whether they could stay. While they waited for a decision to be made, the asylum seekers were brought to the church to stay. If they had family or friends living in the country, the church would help them be reunited.

Shadow Rock had an agreement with a government agency called ICE, or Immigration and Customs Enforcement, that ICE would bring people to the church for shelter, and neither the church nor ICE would tell anyone. This was to keep the asylum seekers safe, so no one would come to the church to make trouble.

But then one day in 2018, ICE showed up at the church with two busloads of asylum seekers from Central America. There were 104 of them! Pastor Ken and his congregation were confused, because reporters showed up at the church too. Ken asked the reporters, "Why are you here? How did you know about the immigrants?" "ICE told us," the reporters replied. ICE had broken their agreement for secrecy. The government wanted people to think that terrible things were happening at the border and that too many people were trying to get into the country. Because it wasn't a secret place anymore, Shadow Rock could no longer safely provide shelter for people seeking asylum.

Pastor Ken is frustrated and sad about the way immigrants are being treated. "Migration is a natural human event," he says. "It is not a criminal activity. The immigrants are trying to escape violence. We need to be a voice in the process. We can't let politicians control it. We are sacrificing peace*making* for peace*keeping*."

Lois Mary Gunden Clemens

Righteous Among the Nations

Twelve-year-old Ginette Drucker and her mother ran onto the train. It was 1942, in the middle of the dark days of World War II. Ginette had just seen her father arrested and taken away to Auschwitz, a German death camp for Jews. Ginette and her mother hid from the men who took her father, then snuck on a train to escape to the south of France. Before they reached their destination, they were caught and taken to Rivesaltes, another death camp, this one in France.

Lois Gunden, a French teacher from Goshen, Indiana, was living and working nearby. She heard about Ginette. She approached Ginette's mother at the camp and begged her to let Ginette come with her. She would be safer at her school, Lois explained. Ginette's mother did not want to part with her daughter, but finally decided it would be best.

Lois smuggled Ginette from the camp and enrolled her at her school.

"At the time I was twelve years old and certainly scared," Ginette Drucker Kalish recalls, "but Lois Gunden was quite kind and passionately determined to take me and these other Jewish children out of Rivesaltes to protect them from harm. . . . She made a special effort to blend us in with the other children. None of the other children were told that we were Jewish."

The school was a French children's home created to help Spanish refugees and Jewish children who were smuggled out of Rivesaltes. Lois had left her job as a professor at Goshen College and moved to France, where she worked with Mennonite Central Committee and a French agency to create this safe place for children.

Lois had to be brave and resourceful in those treacherous times. One day the children were out for a walk when a policeman came to the door. He wanted to arrest three of the Jewish children. Lois told him the children were not there, and would not be back until noon. He returned at noon, and Lois said they were still gone. He said she must pack their clothes and get them ready to go with him when they returned. Lois told him the children's clothes were being washed and would not be dry until later. He left again, and Lois wrote in her journal that she spent the day praying for wisdom, guidance, and safety for the children. The officer never returned, and the children were able to leave with their uncle, who came for them two days later.

Lois continued to run the school, but was eventually arrested by German authorities. They kept her in jail for a year, but eventually released her as part of a prisoner exchange.

She spoke of her time in France in a letter to her mother:

> My year's experience in relief work over here has taught me more than ever that one has to live only a day at a time, and that God's faithfulness towards those who put their trust in Him can be counted upon for the experiences of each day as it comes bringing its particular problems. I know that without the assurance of His abiding presence and His sustaining help, I would feel lost in an impossible tangle of circumstances.

In 2013, Yad Vashem, a world center for research and writing about the Holocaust, recognized Lois Mary Gunden Clemens as Righteous Among the Nations for courageously risking her own life to save children during World War II. She is only the fourth American to ever receive this honor.

Joshua Williams

A kid who helps kids

*J*oshua Williams was four years old when he saw a man with a sign: Need Food. He didn't understand how that could be. "In America, kids aren't shown that people are hungry," he says now. "It was really revealing to me that people out there need help."

But . . . at four years old? What could he do?

"Every day," his mother says, "he would ask, 'Mom, can we do something to help? I want to make a difference.' A lot of times parents or the adults don't listen. We think, oh, they don't know what they're talking about or they're not serious. But he was persistent."

Joshua began looking for an organization that would allow children to help. He couldn't find any. He and his mom started by helping a few families at his grandmother's church, but the need was so great that they decided to start their own foundation, Joshua's Heart.

"When I started the foundation," Joshua says, "I made sure my priority was to get kids to help kids. I started out with my family and some close friends helping out, and eventually my friends told their friends, and those friends told their friends, and it just expanded really quickly."

Joshua's Heart has several different ways that they distribute food. People can come to the pantry every week to get a bag of food. Schoolchildren receive bags with meals to take home for the weekend. And Joshua and his friends also hand out boxes of food and toiletries to people who are homeless and living on the streets of South Florida. One of the recipients was heard to say that Joshua isn't just providing food—he's providing hope.

So far, Joshua's Heart has distributed over 2.2 million pounds of food. They have helped over 450,000 people! But Joshua is the first to say you don't have to start big. "If you can't feed one hundred, feed one," he says. "Just start small—help out your neighbor. Whether it's walking the dog or mowing the lawn for free, something like that." He believes that if you start small and get others involved, eventually you can have a big influence on the lives of others.

Joshua believes one of the key things that made his foundation grow was to get people his age involved. His charity has more than 25,000 volunteers, and over half of them are kids! Joshua encourages other youth to see there is something more to life than staying home and playing video games. Helping others is what's real. Kids might drag their feet at first, but they quickly see they can make a difference. All their hard work pays off when they see the people's smiles.

Many of Joshua's friends have gone on to start their own foundations or projects, whether it's raising money to feed Mayan and Guatemalan families or distributing blankets or children's books. "I think passing on the torch and lighting a new flame in another person to do good is probably one of the bigger missions I have," Joshua says. "I found my purpose in life and my passion in life, which is to help those who are in need. I also must thank God for showing me one of my passions. He allowed me to be able to help others and to learn the value of giving. Everything I am and everything I have experienced is because of God's will and his plan for me. Every day I wake up, I'm grateful to be in the position that I am in."

Linda and Millard Fuller

Homebuilders

*B*eau, Emma, and their five children lived in a shack. The shack had no insulation. It could be either very cold or very hot. It also had no plumbing, so there were no indoor bathrooms or sinks. They needed a new home!

Around the same time, a couple named Linda and Millard Fuller worked at a community farm called Koinonia. Millard had been a lawyer and made a lot of money, but he and Linda were not happy. They decided to sell everything they had, give their money to the poor, and find a new mission for their life. What they found was Koinonia Farm. The farm was owned by a Bible teacher named Clarence Jordan.

Together with Clarence Jordan, the Fullers got an idea that they called "partnership housing." This meant people in need of a home could work side-by-side with volunteers to build a decent, affordable house where they could live. Beau and Emma, the people who lived in the shack, were the first to build a home in this program. They moved into a house with a nice kitchen, indoor bathrooms, and a working heating system!

In 1973, Millard and Linda took their idea, which they called "The Fund for Humanity," to Zaire, now the Democratic Republic of Congo, in Africa, with the Disciples of Christ church. They worked for three years until the program launched and houses were being built. Then they came back to the United States. They brought together supporters to talk about their dream of becoming Habitat for Humanity International.

Habitat believes that every person has the right to live in a safe shelter. There are many people who have a hard time making house payments or rent. Many people live in dangerous neighborhoods, in damaged or run-down buildings, or in homes that are too small for the number of people using them. People who come to Habitat not only end up with a good house, but also put in many hours of work, so when they move in they know they did a lot of it themselves. This helps people feel pride in their home, and gives them a sense of strength and independence.

Habitat also helps people who want to pay for their homes but struggle to find the money. Habitat volunteers offer loans that are paid back in smaller amounts than at a regular bank. The lenders do not charge interest, because of the verse from Exodus 22:25: "If you lend money to my people who are poor among you, don't be a creditor and charge them interest." This compassionate way of loaning money makes it possible for loans to be paid off, and for people to own their own homes.

Within Habitat, Linda created a program called Women Build. Women are most often the people who end up living in unsafe homes. Women Build gives women the opportunity to learn about construction. Even if a woman has no experience, she is welcome to volunteer, make new friends, and help other women move into one of the Habitat homes.

As of today, there are Habitat homes in fourteen hundred communities across the United States. There are also homes in seventy different countries! Habitat for Humanity has helped more than thirteen million people move into safe, low-cost housing.

Seeking to put God's love into action, Habitat for Humanity brings people together to build homes, communities, and hope. Their dream is to help create a world where everyone has a decent place to live.

Frank Albrecht

Mediator

I am a peacemaker at McCaskey High School." That's how Frank Albrecht describes himself. "I pray in the morning that God would bring people my way who are in crisis and may need my help."

Back in 1990, Frank was working as a health and physical education teacher in Lancaster, Pennsylvania, when five of his students got into a fight after school. What do you think caused this fight? One of them spilled soup on another's varsity letter jacket! In the fight, one of the boys stabbed another one, almost hitting his heart. The student nearly died.

Frank decided he needed to do something to help students work out problems in a better way. "That incident woke up something in me," he says. "Five boys' lives were changed forever because they responded to a conflict with violence instead of working it out peacefully."

The administrators at Frank's school agreed. They said he could start a peer mediation program and train students to help. Mediation means bringing people together to talk through their problems to find a good solution. Often, if people can listen to each other's side of an issue, they can find a peaceful solution instead of feeling that they have to fight. "I see my role here as bringing harmony to our campus," Frank says.

Every day at the school, there are students "on duty" during each class period, ready to help if conflicts come up. There are thirty-two student mediators, and they conduct three hundred and fifty-five mediations each school year! Frank himself also works with large groups of students, students and teachers who have issues, or parents and their children who have difficult challenges, to help them work through their problems peacefully.

Frank works with the peer mediators every week to help them see the best ways to assist other students. He says, "I ask them about the conflicts in their own lives too; to be sure they are walking the talk of peaceful relationships."

Frank took his experience to many other local high schools that were interested in starting peer mediation programs. He also worked with Mennonite Central Committee in Colombia, South America, helping schools start mediation programs there, and trained fourth- and fifth-grade mediators at Martin Luther King Elementary School in his city. Now he is back at McCaskey, and the mediation program is thriving!

McCaskey is also training students to simply listen to each other. Students do close to one thousand peer "listenings" per year. "As peer listeners, they aren't counselors or problem solvers," Frank says. "The peer listener just listens to the student who wants to talk about whatever challenge they're facing. They ask questions, and they provide a safe and encouraging space for the student to figure out for themselves what they want to do. It's incredibly meaningful and empowering. We have some students who are dealing with painful, incredibly difficult issues in their lives. Unbelievable issues. When they come to school, they bring all of that with them. As adults, working with them, teaching them, I think our biggest job is that we have to keep hope alive for them. Teaching them peaceful ways to work through conflict is just one way to do that. Listening, really listening, to them is another."

Frank's dream is to put peer mediation programs in every school. He knows this is a big dream, but he believes that it's important. He says, "Creating harmony and keeping hope alive for every student. That's what we should be all about."

Lucy Roca Caballero

Church planter

Lucy Roca Caballero is a pastor and church planter in Quebec. She has started Spanish-speaking house churches in Canada and works for the Mennonite church. But before she made her way to Canada, she lived in Colombia, in South America, where she had to overcome many challenges to get where she is today.

Lucy always knew she wanted to serve God, but she was not sure how. For a while she thought she might be a nun, but decided not to, because she wanted a family. She got married and had three daughters and decided that she would serve God by helping those around her. She and her husband started an organization that worked for women's rights and to prevent violence in the home. They would make complaints to the police when people got hurt or were threatened.

At the time, Lucy and her family were living in the city of Bogotá, where they met people from the Mennonite church. She saw how the church worked for justice, social issues, community building, and nonviolence. She believed in all these same things, and promised to work with them. She and her family lived in Bogotá for two years.

But in 2000, Lucy's brother was killed by terrorists in her hometown of Barranquilla. Her mother and siblings applied for asylum—a safe place to live—and were accepted to move to Canada. But Lucy and her husband decided to stay in Colombia. They thought they would be safe if they moved back to Barranquilla.

Lucy went back to school to study social work. She became the coordinator for a group that worked to help people in the city who were in danger or homeless. This group worked with several other organizations. She was asked to be the coordinator of them all, but she felt God telling her not to do this. Later, the new coordinator was arrested, and an arrest warrant was put out for all people working with him.

Lucy kept serving in her group, but it was very dangerous. Some of her coworkers were arrested, or even killed. She knew it wasn't safe to be working against the government. Even though she believed that she was doing what was right, she was scared.

A pastor came to see her and prayed for her. The pastor told her not to be afraid, because God had called her to this important work and would protect her.

This gave Lucy hope and courage, but she was still afraid. People told her she was in danger and that she should leave Barranquilla. She decided to go to Bogotá to work with the Mennonite church again. She also applied for asylum in Canada. It took two years for the paperwork to be approved. During that time she stayed with the Mennonites and moved around frequently so she would not be found by people wanting to harm her. It was in those years that she felt even more that she was doing God's work. The Mennonites saw her service and asked if she would become a pastor when she was able to move to Canada.

Finally, her family's application was accepted. They moved to Canada, where she now helps other immigrants. "We have to be concerned about each other," she says. "And follow Jesus. The most important thing is to persevere at the hand of the Lord, even when there are moments of great, small, or discouraging opposition, physically or spiritually. . . . The Lord calls us, he affirms, and he confirms he is with us."

Jeremiah Chico

Reihe Einen musician

*J*eremiah Chico was four years old when he fell in love with the violin. He picked up an instrument that belonged to someone at church, and the bond was made. As a toddler, he was always singing at home, and the violin became one more avenue for his love of music.

In elementary school, things grew difficult. Bullies found him to be an easy target. Music was his only outlet. When he got to junior high, he found a way to deal with the bad times. He brought together some of his musician friends to form a supportive group. They call themselves Reihe Einen.

"I founded the group to help build bridges across people of different backgrounds," Jeremiah says. "Each member is of a different religious, ethnic, and academic background. I often refer to the group as 'the outcast group' because we all have dealt with our share of discrimination and grief from society." Members have experienced bullying, exclusion, and abuse.

Reihe Einen, which means "row one" in German, plays classical music. Playing together is meaningful, and the group offers a safe space to belong. "I do the best I can to support them, and they do the best they can to support one another," says Jeremiah. "We are more like a family and less like an ensemble."

Besides supporting each other, the ensemble uses their music to help others. In the fall of 2018 they had a concert to raise money for relief kits for Mennonite Central Committee. These kits consist of items needed by refugees in other countries: towels, toothbrushes, soap, and other hygiene items people need to be healthy. Other organizations to benefit from Reihe Einen's fundraisers are St. Jude Children's Research Hospital and the Interfaith Hospitality Network, which offers temporary housing for families who don't have homes.

Benefit concerts are a way for Jeremiah to give back. He says, "Oftentimes it is so easy to close yourself off from the world, but in my experience, if I listen to God and let her words go in one ear and out the other in not giving back, then I am just as bad as those who have wronged me. If I cannot do what I can to give to others, what is there? The greatest gift you can give is love, and we put our hearts and souls into our music. God knows too well that this world needs more love."

Jeremiah's grandmother Naomi Chapman is proud of what Jeremiah has accomplished. "He is the director and organizer, but works at highlighting the other kids," she says. "He wants to encourage other teens to keep working at the potential they have."

But Jeremiah doesn't see himself as some sort of superman. He's just someone trying to make a difference with his gifts. "I'm a regular Joe," he says. "I'm a person who loves music, and it's my whole life, and my calling from God."

Jeremiah sees his past and tries to view it as God would wish. He says, "Being a peacemaker is about loving. Not yourself, but others. I, personally, cannot say that I hate anyone. I love people, but I may not always like them. People do bad things, but that's no reason for us to do things in retaliation that 'equalize' the wrong. If we can't love, then we cannot have any hope of fixing this world. After all, love was, and is, the greatest commandment. My group loves music, and has learned how to love each other for their differences."

Carolyn Schrock-Shenk

Peace professor

Carolyn Schrock-Shenk was an athlete. She loved to run. She participated in all kinds of sports. But when she was a senior in college, all that changed. She was in a car accident that broke several bones in her back. "I was told I miraculously escaped paralysis," she said. "I said then that it was because God knew I couldn't handle life in a wheelchair."

For many years she was able to move and walk, just not as well as before. She worked as a missionary and a mediator with Mennonite Central Committee, bringing people together to talk through their problems and find good solutions. Finally, she took a job teaching peace, justice, and conflict studies at Goshen College. But after a while her body started to fail. She was faced with a decision—should she have surgery to try to repair the damage in her back, or should she accept the way her body was changing? She decided to have the surgery. It did not go as she hoped. After a few painful years she ended up paralyzed below her chest. She had to live with a wheelchair after all.

It was not easy to accept the changes in her life. The next years were filled with grief and sadness as she wished for the life she used to live. When she was trying to decide what to do next, she said she would not go back to teaching if she had to teach from a wheelchair. "Now here I am," she said about her tough choices. "Peacemaking has become a very personal thing—trying to make peace with what life has handed me. While I have come a long way, I will never be completely done grieving. There are times when I am suddenly filled with an intense longing for the body and life I once had."

After two difficult years, Carolyn returned to teaching—in a wheelchair. Her students were happy to see her, and she had much to teach about peacemaking. Besides teaching students how to handle conflict with others, she also had experience dealing with inner struggles. She was used to being independent, living life with lots of energy, and taking risks. She felt she was no longer the person she used to be. "Now I am having to learn the hard lesson of being helped day after day," she said, "And I'm very grateful for a supportive family, church, and campus community that is making the learning easier."

She was able to get back to bicycling by using a bike with hand pedals. A van was also changed so she could drive, using hand controls. This allowed her to run errands, drive to church, and take her sons to their activities.

Even with these new tools, life was challenging. But amid these challenges, Carolyn came to understand that

God could help her find good things in her life and bring good things to others, even if it was a life that was very different from what she had planned.

Carolyn died in 2019. She is missed by everyone who knew and loved her. They remember the lessons she taught them about making peace with each other and finding peace in life's circumstances. Sometimes life makes it almost impossible to accept the problems you are given, but even with struggles you can live as a peacemaker.

Elisante Daniel Lulu

Social media peacemaker

*E*lisante Daniel Lulu is a Christian from Tanzania, a country in eastern Africa. Christians make up about 61 percent of the country's population. Muslims are the next largest religious group, with about 35 percent of the people. Sometimes it's hard for people from these different beliefs to get along. In July 2015, relationships between the two religions were tense.

"Some Christian churches suffered attacks," Elisante says, "especially in Zanzibar, an island off Tanzania's coast. In Zanzibar the population is 90 percent Muslim. That area tended to be more violent against Christians, more challenging. And sometimes there was violence even in the northern part, in Mwanza. In these instances, someone who went to church was killed, or the church and everything in it was burned by unknown people. But we usually knew that it was a group of people with different religious beliefs."

Elisante wanted to stop this violence by talking with people, so that they could see things from others' points of view. He interacted a lot on social media. He also met with people in person to talk. He went to groups that were both Muslim and Christian, where they discussed their faith together. Sometimes it was challenging to talk with people who thought differently. People on the other side of conversations often got angry and said things that were unkind. Elisante especially found this when he was involved in social media discussions.

"When the Muslims there would use violent words," he says, "sometimes the Christians became defensive. I saw that some Christians could also be violent, using the same kind of language. So the arguments would just escalate. But I soon realized that nonviolent words would cool down the situation. Whenever the other side would use violent and aggressive language, I would use very polite words. Many times I would say, 'I really love what you said and I understand what you say. And I really love you.' I would say this even though they were very angry towards the Christians."

Elisante found that responding to anger and hatred with kindness could stop violent language in its tracks. Now he holds workshops and teaches people how to create a safer space for talking together. He finds that speaking with love and understanding can calm people down quickly, whether on social media or in person.

Elisante knows there is more than one side to every story. He wants Christians to see that everything is not the fault of the Muslims. "I do not blame the Islamic religion,"

Elisante says, "because we have many, many Islamic friends who are very helpful to us. We work together, we eat together. We can eat from the same plate or drink from the same cup. We share a lot of things. But we do have a lot of differences. Even among Christians this is true. Some are very conservative, some are open-minded. So whenever we have misunderstandings, we must come and sit and talk together. We may have differences, but our differences become less and less as we talk."

Elisante believes that if we show love and kindness to people, even if those people do not act with the same gentleness, others will see how thoughtful words can make change. It will lead to peace between people who are very different from each other.

"If we love the people who don't believe as we believe," he says, "it will show love. If we demonstrate actions of peace and love, they will want to know what we believe."

Olivia Wright
Shoe provider

*O*livia Wright was nine years old when she saw a commercial for the organization Feed the Children. She was upset to realize the children on the television were not wearing shoes. They had bare feet and sad faces! These children were living so close to her home in Nashville, Tennessee. How was it that they didn't have any shoes?

She went to her parents and told them she wanted to do something to help these children. After some discussion, her parents agreed to help her. Together, they would make something happen.

Olivia organized a shoe drive at her church. She collected over 650 pairs! Olivia wanted to not only give the children shoes, but make a personal connection with them. So she traveled to Appalachia with the shoes and met the children there.

After this first drive, Olivia didn't want to stop. She founded H.U.G.S., which stands for Help Us Give Shoes.

Their motto is "Shoeing the world, one smile at a time!" Olivia doesn't want to stop until everyone can walk with their feet protected. She started with the kids, but then realized that adults needed shoes too.

"We live in a place where shoes are a necessity," Olivia says. "Without shoes many children are denied the ability to go to school, have the possibility of dangerous penetration in their feet, and are susceptible to many life-affecting diseases, bacteria, and parasites. By giving children and adults shoes, we are not only keeping them safe; we're also showing them that they are loved and that someone somewhere cares about them enough to provide them with something they so desperately need."

In the years since H.U.G.S. began, Olivia and her organization have given away more than one hundred thousand pairs of shoes. Olivia's mission began in the Appalachian mountains, and she continues to deliver shoes there twice a year. But Olivia is passionate about making sure to "shoe" many places in the United States. So she goes on as many local "shoeing" trips as she can. "It's more than meeting a need for shoes," she says. "It's about letting people know that someone does genuinely care. God cares. We care."

But the giving doesn't stop in the United States. H.U.G.S. has taken shoes all over the world to such countries as Russia, Nicaragua, India, Kenya, Uganda, Zimbabwe, Haiti, and the Dominican Republic! The organization has also expanded into disaster relief all over the world. They recently held a shoe and coat drive for people in Florida dealing with the effects of Hurricane Michael. H.U.G.S. was also asked specifically for hygiene items, diapers, baby wipes, new blankets, towels, and sleeping bags.

When asked what someone can do to make a difference, Olivia encourages everyone to find what makes sense for them. "I think the number one advice I can give is to be passionate," she says. "Find what you think needs to be changed, what tugs at your heartstrings, and change it! Peace is possible, but it is up to us to make it a reality. I want you to know that you are capable of things—amazing, extraordinary, and powerful things! You and I currently live in a world of endless possibilities. With hard work and determination we can unlock those possibilities and create an amazing outcome. Remember to have hope, faith, and love. Don't be afraid to ask for help, and believe in yourself. Also, use social media, the media, and the Internet. That's my quick tidbit on how you can make a difference!"

Siegfried Bartel

Soldier turned pacifist

*I*n 1937, near the beginning of World War II, Siegfried Bartel felt that God wanted him to serve as an officer in the German army. Every young man, including the ones at his church, were joining up. But soon after he joined it was Christmas Eve, and as he sat with his soldiers in a trench near the Russian border, he wasn't so sure. What was he doing in that freezing cold trench? Was that really where God wanted him? Did God want him out there, ready to kill the enemy?

"Captain!" one of his soldiers whispered. "Listen!"

Siegfried went still. He could hear one of the Russian soldiers talking to his comrades on the other end of a radio. Siegfried closed his eyes and listened as hard as he could. Perhaps he would hear the soldiers talking about battle plans. Siegfried could find out what the enemy was up to.

But Siegfried was stunned. The soldiers weren't talking about battle—they were singing! Siegfried couldn't believe his ears. The Russian soldiers—the enemy!—were singing Christmas carols! The same Christmas songs Siegfried sang back home with his family. The same songs that spoke of Jesus being born. How could this be?

Siegfried began to think differently about the Russians. They were people too. People with families and friends and homes they loved, just like Siegfried! Perhaps God had a different plan for Siegfried after all.

At the end of the war, Siegfried and his family lost their home. Mennonite Central Committee, or MCC, was helping with relief efforts in Germany, and they took care of the Bartel family. Siegfried took great interest in the Mennonites' ideas about pacifism, which means nonviolence. When Siegfried was a young boy, his mother and brother were killed in an accident. A man who was intoxicated made a mistake, causing a train to hit the car that was carrying Siegfried's family. Siegfried remembered his father granting forgiveness to the man. Now, it seemed, God wanted Siegfried to love his enemy, too, and work for peace.

"Our forefathers' interpretation of Matthew 5, to love your enemy, was right to include people on the other side of the border," Siegfried said. "The state has no right to tell me whom I should love and who will be my enemy."

Siegfried and his wife, Erna, moved from their home in Prussia to Canada. Siegfried worked as a dairy farmer, but he also worked for Mennonite Central Committee. He wanted to help all people who needed someone to stand up for them: people with mental disabilities, Indigenous people, people who were homeless, refugees, and people oppressed by their governments. Everyone who knew him was impressed by how much he cared about others and how important the message of peace was to him.

"A life of peace is actually the message of Christianity, and we have neglected that in our home, in our families, in our society, even in our churches," Siegfried said. "We must take Jesus' message to love everybody much more seriously than we do. If we would live a life of peace every moment of our lives, we could change society."

Siegfried did change the world around him through the love he showed to everyone. A lot of it was because of that cold Christmas Eve when he realized the soldiers on the other side of the war were not truly his enemies, not in God's eyes. "My pacifism," he said, "which I cherish so much today, may have been born at that moment."

Maria Rose Belding

Food organizer

When Maria Rose Belding was fourteen, she worked in her church's food pantry in her small Iowa town. "Jesus said, 'For I was hungry and you fed me,'" she says. "Stacking cans was my answer to this call."

As she worked, she realized there were serious issues with the way the system worked. "You would have way too much of one thing and be in desperate need of a different thing," she says. "Inevitably some of it would expire. I'd end up throwing a lot of it away. How can there be forty million people going hungry and up to 40 percent of the food supply going to waste? That's such an obvious thing to fix."

One day the food pantry was given a huge amount of macaroni and cheese that was ready to eat, but there weren't enough people in her community to use it all. Maria tried to contact other charities, but it was difficult to make connections.

"I remember just crying and being so angry," Maria says. "There was nothing that really allowed us to communicate in an efficient way." She was frustrated, particularly because she knew the Internet was right in front of them.

Maria decided that with online possibilities, there was no reason she couldn't try a different system. While in high school, she created the MEANS Database. MEANS stands for Matching Excess and Need for Stability. What that really means is exactly what Maria set out to do—make it easy for people who have extra food to get it to people who need it.

Maria had the database, but didn't have the tech knowledge to make it go live. When she got to college, she met another student named Grant Nelson, who knew how to write code. Working together, they launched the free online platform where Maria's dream of helping to feed the hungry came true.

Here's how it works. Restaurants, caterers, and grocery stores log onto the database and input how much extra food they have, what it is, and when it needs to be picked up. A text goes out to charities—food pantries and soup kitchens—that can claim however much they need. Someone from the charity picks up the food and, within minutes, can have that food on the table of hungry people. "We are a digital bridge," Maria says, "between excess food and the people in need. It should be easier to give food to people in need than to ditch it in a dumpster."

Maria can't hide her enthusiasm for the project. She says, "You'd think the novelty would wear off—nope! In our office, every time you see a donation go live on our admin panel, and then you see somebody has claimed it, you're like, 'It worked!' When you see food move, you know that that's people getting to eat who maybe wouldn't have been able to—or maybe they're getting to eat better than they would have. You're also keeping food from going to landfills. It's just great for everybody."

The MEANS team is made up of mostly teens and college students. The mission speaks to them and catches them where their interests lie—helping hungry people, as well as the Internet. Working together and partnering with charities and food retailers, they found a home for over 2.1 million pounds of food in the first three years of the database.

"What makes it worth it," Maria says, "is we're building something that matters a lot more than we do."

Mike Martin

Blacksmith

Mike Martin was a youth and young adult pastor in the mountains of Colorado when the words of Isaiah 2:4 swirled around and around in his head.

They will beat their swords into iron plows

and their spears into pruning tools.

Nation will not take up sword against nation;

they will no longer learn how to make war.

What was God telling him? What would it look like if someone really did beat weapons into tools? Mike began talking to friends and mentors about the possibilities. He wanted to make this happen. The Beth-El Mennonite congregation and the Mountain States region of the church rallied around him, supporting him through events, prayer, and money. He learned how to blacksmith, which is the actual work needed to transform the guns, and formed an organization called RAWtools.

RAWtools travels around the country. People bring their guns to the RAWtools forge, and the staff take the weapons, heat them up, and hammer them into tools like garden spades or hoes. The process is loud and hot and satisfying. Each weapon-turned-tool even gets its own story, so the donor can see how the tool is being used.

It's easy to find people arguing for different sides of the gun issue—we need more guns to protect ourselves, or we need to get rid of all guns. RAWtools sees the work of beating swords into plows as a symbol. Mike and his staff turn weapons into tools. It doesn't mean everyone needs to be a gardener or farmer, but their work shows that we can all do something to benefit the larger community.

"The example of Jesus gives us so much," Mike says, "especially in the Sermon on the Mount." In the book of Matthew, this is the first time we read words that Jesus spoke to a crowd. There, Jesus gives us guidelines to be peacemakers, to comfort those who mourn, and to show mercy. Mike believes that we should spend more time looking at our world through the Sermon on the Mount. "Our choices in life always affect more than just ourselves," he says. "Many of us have the ability to make choices that help everyone around us and not just 'me.'"

Mike tells the story of one man who brought in a gun: "Our first gun donor gave us an AK-47. While that was a big deal in itself, five years later he also gave us his handgun. The AK-47 was given in response to the shooting at Sandy Hook Elementary School, and the handgun was given to mark the fifth anniversary of Sandy Hook. I like this donor's story because it represents a journey he has taken, and breaks down stereotypes some have of gun owners. He still owns some guns for hunting, but has clearly decided his handgun and AK-47 were not worth the risk of owning."

RAWtools helps people learn to treat each other with kindness, no matter how different they are. "Listening to the stories of those around us, our neighbors and our enemies, family and friends, has to happen if we want to end gun violence," Mike says. "I've learned it's a gun problem and a heart problem, and we have to decide that we will never hurt each other, nor allow the tools, like guns, to be a part of our conflict resolution. The way forward will not be comfortable, but it will cultivate life. That's what choosing a plow over a sword asks of us."

Tonja Murphy

Ladybug Club mentor

*T*onja Murphy loved spending time with her teenage daughter and preteen nieces, but she wanted their time together to be more than just "hanging out." She wanted their hours filled with worthwhile activities, conversation, and love. She wanted them to spend time with people who would teach them self-esteem, self-confidence, the value of education, and a deep love for their family and community. So she created a space for that to happen.

The Ladybug Club, named for Tonja's daughter, whose nickname is Ladybug, became that safe and wonderful space. Tonja brought together other women who also believed in this mission—mothers, grandmothers, aunts, and mentors from her church and community.

Tonja began holding Ladybug Club meetings in her home, but the group soon grew so big that they had to move to Northminster Baptist Church, where Tonja is a member. The women and girls get together there to talk about all sorts of things, like health and hygiene, school projects, dating, and friendship. They also attend events and participate in community service. Some of their projects have included care packages for women who are in prison, support for the elderly, and Lemonade Day, where they host lemonade stands and donate the money to worthy causes.

What makes the Ladybug Club so special? The relationships between the girls and the women. Tonja wants the girls to feel that they have somewhere they can talk about things that are important to them. The girls in the club come from all sorts of backgrounds. Single- and double-parent homes, different financial situations, and a variety of neighborhoods. But no matter where they come from, Tonja wants to offer them additional "moms" who can be a part of their lives.

"We encourage the girls to have strong relationships with their moms," Tonja says. "We know that is so important . . . but there also are times where maybe the mom just isn't comfortable talking about certain things, or they have already talked about it and just feel like they aren't getting through. Another mom can be there to step in and listen or give advice."

Paige, a young member of the Ladybug Club, says, "It's really taught me how to get out of my comfort zone. It challenges me to do different things and also to speak out. I talk more at school now and I give my opinions more because I've been taught to do that."

Paige's mother is also grateful for the organization. She sees that our world can be petty and mean, and the Ladybug

Club offers a space where her daughter can be encouraged and learn to make positive choices.

The Ladybug Club helps the girls look ahead, to see the possibilities for their lives. The group has the opportunity to hear from guest speakers who have different careers, goals, and family experiences. "We teach them there is a lot to being a woman," Tonja says about the guest speakers she invites. "We talk about how women have to learn to take care of others, but also to take care of themselves and to treat themselves well."

The Ladybug Club started out small but has grown into something that enriches not only the lives of the girls but also their community. With the help of their moms and mentors, these teens and preteens are learning how to love themselves, and the world around them.

Miles Lin

Aquaponics fisherman

Ever since Miles Lin was three years old, he's had a passion for one thing—fish. He loves fishing with his grandpa and mom, and he loves eating the fish he catches. He even convinced his younger brother, who doesn't like seafood, that if he catches a fish, he has to eat it! But one thing his parents taught him is this: Your passions aren't meant only for yourself. You must share them with the rest of the world.

When Miles was nine, he learned some difficult facts. One in six children in the developing world is underweight. That's 101 million children. One in nine people goes to bed hungry. That means 805 million people don't have enough to eat. Miles never had to think about being hungry. In fact, he threw away food he didn't want! So he wondered . . . how could he use fish—something he loves—to feed some of these starving people?

Miles researched fish farms, and found a professor at a local university who used a system called aquaponics. Aquaponics is a type of growing operation where two different life forms—fish and plants—work together. Fish live at the bottom of a large tank, and a vegetable garden grows on the top. The nutrient-rich water from the lower part of the water (or "poop water," as Miles likes to say!) fertilizes the plants growing on the top. The plants recycle the water and send fresh water down to the fish. Fifteen hundred fish can live in one tank, and can feed an entire school of children!

Miles and his parents decided this could be a great way to feed people who are hungry and don't have the resources they need. Miles began a charity called I Dream of Fish, whose mission is to solve world hunger, one fish at a time. Miles and his parents organized a fundraiser. People in their church and community came out to support the dream, and they raised enough to begin building their first aquaponics fish tank in Tenali, India. Since then, Miles has held more fundraisers so they can build more fish tanks in India, and also start aquaponics projects in Uganda.

Miles found out that people in Haiti also needed food. Haiti is the poorest country in the Western Hemisphere, and 30 percent of its people don't have enough to eat. Miles wanted to take his fish farms to them. However, when he began talking to the Haitian people, they said fish would not be very popular there. What they really needed was chickens! Rather than force his own passion for fish on the Haitians, Miles and I Dream of Fish worked with one community to start a chicken farm. The farm has five hundred chickens, and produces over three thousand eggs a week! This sustainable farm provides not only food but also much-needed jobs.

In 2017, I Dream of Fish also began working in Cambodia. The farm there has fish, frogs, and chickens. The locals love eating frogs! When Miles visited the community over spring break, he made sure to try some frog. A different experience!

Miles continues to work with I Dream of Fish to feed a hungry world. The organization works with experts and people who live within the community to make sure that what they are doing is both helpful and sustainable. Miles wishes for true and hopeful change so that people can live happy and healthy lives.

Preacher Peter and Anna

Folks who fed their enemies

One night, way back in the 1700s, a man named Preacher Peter was asleep when he heard noises above his head. "Am I imagining things?" he wondered. But no, he heard it again. Something—or someone—was messing with his house.

Peter was concerned. As a Mennonite preacher, he was having some troubles in his town. He preached about peace and love in a way the people in his small Swiss town didn't always appreciate. He said Jesus wanted us to love our enemies. Jesus didn't want us to respond with violence and hatred. Had someone come to his house to make trouble because of the things he was saying?

Peter got out of bed, lit a lantern, and went outside. Sure enough, there were men on the roof of his house, trying to break in. He prayed for God to give him wisdom. What should he do? What should he say? He got an idea.

Peter ran back into the house and woke his wife, Anna.[1] "There are men on our roof!" he said. "I know this might sound strange, but would you be willing to make a meal for them?"

Anna immediately knew what was going on, and agreed to his plan. She got up, stoked the fire, and cooked food for the people destroying their house. When the meal was ready, Peter went outside and called up to the men. "You must be tired after all that work! Why don't you come down and get something to eat? Rest for a while."

The men were surprised. Peter's invitation didn't make any sense. Unsure what to do, they came down from the roof. Peter led them inside, where Anna had set the table with warm, delicious food. Peter said a simple prayer. "Thank you, God, for the meal you have provided. Thank you also for our guests. Bless them in Jesus' name. Amen."

The men were so shocked and embarrassed they couldn't eat. What was happening? Why was this couple feeding them and treating them as if they were expected company? They should be angry, calling for help. It wasn't normal, the way this couple was acting. The men sat quietly, confused and ashamed.

Finally, the men left the table and went back outside. Peter and Anna heard sounds on the roof. Maybe their plan hadn't worked after all. The men had gone right back to what they were doing. Peter and Anna walked outside, unsure what to do next. They thought they had done what God suggested.

---

1 We don't know the name of Preacher Peter's wife, so we have called her Anna.

When they saw the men back on the top of their house, they weren't sure what was going on. They soon discovered that the men were fixing the holes they had put in the roof. The men had realized that their actions hadn't made Peter and Anna act differently from the peaceful message Peter preached. Anna and Peter had not treated the men with violence and hatred. Instead, they responded with love, kindness, and hospitality.

The men fixed the roof and went away.

"If your enemies are starving," Proverbs 25:21 says, "feed them some bread; if they are thirsty, give them water to drink."

Preacher Peter and Anna walked back inside, and went to sleep.

Bryan Moyer Suderman

Singer-songwriter

*I*t's hard to talk to people about the Bible sometimes. It's even harder to talk to someone when the two of you think very differently about something that's important to you both. Have you ever had that experience? You're talking with a friend about a situation at school, a story you heard on the news, or something you learned at church. Maybe your friend has the opposite viewpoint. Maybe your friend quickly quotes a Bible verse to try to end the conversation.

How should you respond?

Bryan Moyer Suderman is a singer-songwriter from Kitchener, Ontario. He thinks a lot about how we use the Bible. He believes the Bible should not be used as a weapon in conversation. Bryan has become fascinated by the way gospel stories describe Jesus using Scripture (what we call the Old Testament) in his conversations with the people he meets. He wonders how we can read the Bible and come to understand its message for us today, even if it is an ancient book.

Bryan's favorite Bible verse is not one you usually hear people talk about. He thinks Deuteronomy 5:3 has one of the most important messages in the Bible: "Not with our ancestors did the Lord make this covenant, but with us, who are all of us here alive today" (NRSV).

Alive. Here. Today. That's us. When you are playing soccer, you are God's child. When you are singing, or watching a movie, or doing homework, or playing with siblings or friends, you are God's child here, today.

Bryan grew up engaging with the arts. He performed in musicals and sang in middle school. During high school he began really studying the Bible. As an adult he loved both music and the Bible. It became very important to him to make the Bible something everyone could understand. He wanted young people to see that the Bible's mission of peace, justice, and blessing is for everyone, of all ages. He decided to do something about it. He sat down with his three-year-old son and wrote this song:

God's love is for everybody

Everyone around the world

Me and you and all God's children

From across the street to around the world . . .[1]

---

1 Lyrics used with permission from Bryan Moyer Suderman/SmallTall Music (www.smalltallministries.com). "God's Love Is for Everybody" is on the album of the same name (*God's Love Is for Everybody*).

This was just the beginning of Bryan's ministry. Now he travels all over Canada and the United States bringing this message to everyone he can. God's love is for everyone. We are alive here today to spread that love to all the people we meet.

The Bible helps us learn about God's love and how to share it. This is not always easy, and reading the Bible isn't always easy either. Sometimes it's a struggle to make sense of what we read and the best way to show God's love in different situations. Another of Bryan's songs describes this as "wrestling"—wrestling with the Scriptures, with each other, even with God sometimes. The song says that "Jesus was a wrestler" too! Learning about the stories and the "wrestling" in the Bible can help us learn how to act in difficult situations, like when we see someone being bullied or are asked to do something we know is wrong. And we can learn how to live together in a positive way, even if we don't always agree with each other.

Bryan believes we are alive here today to spread God's love. His music and his teaching help others to understand how we can be God's people of peace wherever we are.

Tegla Laroupe

Athlete

*T*egla Laroupe was born in Kenya, the sister to twenty-four siblings. She spent her childhood working in the fields and looking after her younger brothers and sisters. Her nickname was Chametia, which means "the one who never gets annoyed," because she had such a cheerful personality.

When Tegla was seven, she began going to school. She had to run ten kilometers, or about six miles, each way to get there. It was during this time that she realized she was a strong athlete. When she was older, she pursued a running career. Her mother was the only person who supported her running dreams. Tegla did not let this stop her. "In a country where only men are encouraged," Tegla says, "one must be one's own inspiration."

In 1994, Tegla became the first African woman to win the New York City Marathon. After that race, she won many more marathons around the world. With all this success, she decided she must use her fame to promote peace in her country and in the world. She also wanted to share her faith by helping others. "I am a Christian," she says. "I have seen the power of God with me, giving me strength."

In Kenya, a lack of resources causes much conflict. There is not enough water for livestock or farming, which makes it difficult for people to earn a living. This creates tension between tribes, and they sometimes fight or steal cattle, believing this will make things better for themselves and their families.

Tegla saw the violence and crime and wanted to find a way to bring about change. She knew from her own experience that when people get to know each other through sports, they are more likely to talk and work things out in ways other than fighting.

Tegla created the Tegla Laroupe Peace Foundation, which exists to "promote a peaceful, prosperous, and just world in which sports bring people together." Through the foundation, Tegla founded the annual 10K Peace Race in 2006. At the first event, two thousand warriors from six different tribes came together to run. She organizes other Peace Marathons as well, where presidents, prime ministers, ambassadors, and other government officials run with warriors and nomadic groups to try to bring peace to areas plagued by raiding between battling tribes.

Tegla and her foundation also work with the Homeless World Cup, which makes soccer possible for hundreds of thousands of people who otherwise would not have the opportunity to play. "Let us use football and sport to communicate peace, development, and social change," Tegla says.

Thanks to Tegla, the Olympics have also become a place where refugees have an opportunity to compete. Tegla approached the International Olympics Committee and the United Nations Refugee Agency to make participation possible for people who have lost their homes. Now people without a country can compete alongside those who are more fortunate.

Also important to Tegla is her work to bring about awareness of girls' rights and to make education available to all children, no matter their circumstance. She created the Tegla Laroupe Peace Academy, a school for orphans and children from poor families. Here they have the opportunity not only to learn, but to run and participate in other sports. The school offers housing and nutritious food to these children who would not have it otherwise.

Many people see sports as something "extra." Tegla has made it an important part of creating a peaceful world.

Sarah Jebsen

NICU nurse

The nurses in the neonatal intensive care unit, or NICU, at the Blanchard Valley Hospital try to keep the rooms dark and quiet, especially at night. The NICU (pronounced NICK-yoo) is for babies who need extra medical care after they are born. These special babies need a peaceful place to sleep, eat, and get used to life outside their mother's body. They have only a few visitors at a time, and people are asked to keep their voices low.

Some of these special babies were addicted to a drug when they were born because their mother was struggling with addiction while she was pregnant. The NICU nurses hold the babies, sing to them, and swaddle them in blankets to help them feel safe and loved.

Sarah Jebsen is one of these nurses.

She says, "When I graduated from nursing school, I said I will never, ever, ever work with babies." Sarah struggled with depression after one of her children was born, and thought it would be too hard to work with infants. But Sarah made it through her depression, and now she does God's work by helping these little ones who need extra care.

Sarah doesn't only work with the infants. She also forms relationships with the parents. It would be easy to judge the mothers, since they took drugs or smoked while they were pregnant. But Sarah says she sees the parents' pain. Maybe the parents didn't know another way, or maybe they made bad choices. But everyone makes mistakes sometimes.

"These addicted babies don't come from any one group of people," Sarah says. "Struggles affect all of us at one time or another. The moms especially have a hard time when they see their baby and realize how sick it is. They feel ashamed, and embarrassed. They think everyone is judging them." Sarah and her coworkers want to provide hope, and teach the mothers how to take care of their babies and themselves. "Just caring for them and loving them really does make a difference," Sarah says. "Whether it is the baby or the family, if we can love them in a nonjudgmental way, it makes a big impact. Even if we don't see a change while they are with us, my hope is that the parents can look back on the time in the NICU and feel that the staff genuinely cared about them.

Sarah says, "I think about the story of the good Samaritan from the Bible. Unfortunately, I can remember times I've walked by people who were struggling and did not stop to help them. But we look back and learn from our experiences. God has changed my heart since I've been able to develop relationships with patients. This helped me to really stop and look and listen to people's stories, and see where they're coming from. We all have a lot in common. We all have brokenness. God takes that brokenness, and when he brings the pieces together, he makes something beautiful. God is still creating, even out of our struggles."

Sarah spends a lot of time rocking the babies and praying over them. "I believe in the power of prayer," she says. "I just have to put my faith in that. I can't see what will happen to the babies' lives down the road, but God is already there, wherever their path will lead. I whisper in their ears that Jesus loves them. They grasp my fingers and look into my eyes, and I know God is present with us."

Brittany Paris Amano

Aspiring politician

Brittany Paris Amano and her mother were evicted from their home when Brittany was eight years old. They moved into a friend's basement, and Brittany's grandmother had to go to a homeless shelter. During this time they would often go hungry. Brittany didn't let this keep her down. She was inspired by watching her grandmother, who even in the most difficult circumstances continued to give back to everyone who helped her.

In fourth grade, when Brittany was nine, she ran a food drive at her school and gathered over five hundred pounds of food for those in need. Next, she held a walkathon and organized a cookbook. These two fundraisers made over $2,000! She wasn't discouraged by her young age, and didn't let anyone put her off her goals. "Sometimes we shouldn't wait," she says. "Sometimes we should act now."

Brittany wanted to feed more people. She began by serving three hundred people at her church. Eventually, when she was twelve years old, she started the nonprofit Hawaii's Future Isn't Hungry. This organization helps feed people who are homeless and provides school supplies, technology, and Christmas presents for children living in low-income housing. The charity helped so many people that it expanded into The Future Isn't Hungry, which has more than 450 student volunteers and branches in Hawaii, Wisconsin, and Florida.

Besides homelessness and hunger, Brittany also experienced violence in her life. At one point she had to go with her mom and sister to a safe place called a domestic violence shelter, where people go when there is violence at home. As a teenager, Brittany began Teens Stopping Domestic Violence. This organization advocates against violence in the home and teaches teens and adults the early signs of abuse and how to prevent it. They create libraries in domestic violence shelters and collect clothes, toiletries, and other necessities for residents. Brittany's dream is to have a branch of the organization in every state.

Brittany believes you must take your experiences and use them to make the world a better place, as she did with homelessness, hunger, and violence. "Being multiracial also sets me apart. As a minority, a young woman, and someone coming from a family living below the poverty line, people might say that I face many challenges to become a leader," Brittany wrote in an essay. "I see these as what empower me and make me unique."

Brittany is determined to become a politician so she can help the largest number of people. She encourages other young people to use their interests and gifts to help others too. That's what will help our world.

"It doesn't matter if you impact one person or your whole community, raise one dollar or ten million dollars," Brittany says. "Because every small impact counts. After all, you can't reach the million dollar goal without having people helping you collect every single dollar. And it doesn't matter what your passion is. If it's sports, you can hold a sports event and collect pledges. If your passion is art, you can auction off a piece of artwork, or create a piece of art to raise awareness about a cause. If it's performing, you can use your talent to bring smiles to patients at a hospital or perform at a charity fundraiser. I don't care what it is you do, or how good you are at it. All that I care about is that you do something that matters."

Nickel Mines Amish community

Community of forgiveness

In 2006 a troubled man entered the West Nickel Mines Amish schoolhouse in Lancaster County, Pennsylvania. He shot several of the female students before killing himself. This was a tragic day for the school, the community, and the Amish church that the girls attended.

The Amish are a peaceful people who want to live simply and peacefully. Their main source of transportation is horse-drawn buggies. They have no electricity in their homes. Their connections outside their own communities are limited. But even though they live this way, their response to the killings was still not what the rest of the world expected. Many people would have reacted with anger and violence. But instead of speaking words of hate and wanting revenge on the man and his family, the Amish people chose forgiveness.

Members of the Amish community reached out to the widow, parents, and in-laws of the shooter to comfort them on the very first day. They went to see the man's family and said they were sorry about what happened, and that they didn't hold anything against them. One of the Amish men knew the shooter's father because he would drive the Amish places in his vehicle. As the shooter's father cried, the Amish man held him in his arms and told him he forgave him. The Amish church also raised money for the family. About thirty members of the Amish church attended the shooter's funeral, and they invited his widow to the funerals for the murdered students. She was one of only a few non-Amish people allowed to attend.

Some people criticized the Amish community for being so ready to forgive the man for his awful act of violence. But letting go of bitterness is a deeply held belief in Amish culture. Their willingness to forgive has also strengthened their relationship with the outside world. After shootings in other communities, grieving families turned to the Amish community for comfort and advice.

The Nickel Mines Amish community became known as a people who were all about kindness, forgiveness, and love. But while the world saw the choice of forgiveness the Amish community made that day, the decision to forgive the killer and his family was not as simple as it may have appeared.

"It's not a once and done thing," said one of the mothers of the students who was murdered. "It is a lifelong process."

Another church member said, "We still wonder: Why did it happen?" Despite the Amish community's now-famous forgiveness, it's hard for them to always feel forgiving, even though they *choose* it over hatred and revenge. "You have to fight the bitter thoughts," the church member said.

Another man spoke about forgiveness as a journey. He made the immediate choice to forgive on principle, because that was what he believed was right. It was what Jesus would do. But it took him a few years until he truly felt it inside. At the point when he found compassion for the shooter, he felt a great weight fall off him. He felt lighter. He had finally, truly forgiven him, inside and out.

The people of Nickel Mines taught the world an important lesson. While they mourned their lost children, they also sought love and forgiveness. Instead of turning their sorrow into hatred and vengeance, they showed compassion to the family of the shooter. Forgiveness is not simple. It is not easy. But it is the way this community chose to live out its beliefs.

Dr. Sibonokuhle Ncube

Climate change champion

In rural Zimbabwe, in Matabeleland North and South, where Dr. Sibonokuhle Ncube works, there are areas where women and girls have to walk hours to get clean water for their families. There is too little water to grow crops, or too much water at the wrong times, which harms the land and destroys roads, water supplies, and buildings. Climate change makes everyone's life difficult. People fight over resources and live without the things they need.

Dr. Ncube was born in Zimbabwe, a country in southern Africa, and still lives there. She works as the national coordinator of the Brethren in Christ Compassionate and Development Services, a peacebuilding and relief agency. Dr. Ncube believes strongly in helping her country through climate change and developmental problems. "For me, it's a calling," she says. "This is where I think the life of God is—to be and to do as he says." Dr. Ncube says people who live at the margins—those who may be treated poorly or have fewer resources—don't always get the support they need, and the church is working hard to help.

"Climate change is a peace issue," she says. "One day everyone will see that the bad things happening in the southern half of the globe can easily take place in the north if people and governments do not respond with the urgent and necessary attention required." Dr. Ncube also sees that violence and unfair treatment of women and girls has gotten worse because of the lack of food and water. She says, "Communities need help to reduce the food, energy, and water gaps as part of peacemaking." Dr. Ncube wants children to see how they can be a part of this change. She works with students at thirteen different schools to help them understand their peacemaking responsibility to the environment through a "peace tree-athon," where they plant native trees.

Dr. Ncube says climate change is also a peace issue because people are largely responsible for global warming, and for the creation of a world of "haves and have nots." She says, "It is a matter that governments and developers should think through to move communities and the whole world to a cleaner use of resources. Laws and policies need to be made to support farmers and other people who depend on agriculture for their living." One thing Dr. Ncube and her staff do is teach farmers—mostly women—how to mulch crops using grass and leaves. They call this "God's blanket," an idea from a program called Farming God's Way. The mulch keeps moisture in the soil, reduces erosion, and keeps weeds from growing by using cover crops to improve the ground and crop quality, as well as add variety to the crops grown.

"It will take small to big personal changes, such as having smaller families, more efficient refrigeration tools, increasing solar and wind power, and growing more trees," Dr. Ncube says. "Immediate change is important." Her dream is for affordable green solutions that will make better technologies available to everyone. "Even if we are not farmers, and even if we don't feel the effects of climate change on a daily basis, we need to learn about our carbon footprint so we can make better choices," she says. Dr. Ncube wants people to learn how to make healthy decisions for themselves, for their communities, and for the world. She believes we need to create a world of peace that leaves no one behind.

Thad Taylor
Artistic Eagle Scout

*T*had Taylor began his Eagle Scout project three years before the actual ceremony. That's how long it took to create the fifty-six-foot-long mural now adorning the entrance of the Hoops Family Children's Hospital in Huntington, West Virginia. Sometimes people feel nervous when they go to the hospital. Thad wanted to brighten the atmosphere for patients so it wouldn't feel quite so scary.

"I love my community, I love this hospital, and I love making people smile," Thad says. "So I created this welcome wall. I wanted to put smiles on the faces of children and parents who were going through hard times."

The road to putting up the mural wasn't simple. Once Thad had a blueprint, he met with the hospital to show them his idea. It didn't take long for them to approve it, but the area he wanted to use was not available, so he had to rethink his plan. It took about a year from the idea to the start of the work. The hospital staff did their best to help, and Thad made some great friends in the administration. Finally, after the hospital approved the plan, the Boy Scouts of America had to approve it too.

The river scene on the mural is made of 14,000 one-inch glass tiles. The project was huge. First, Thad had to design the mural and the hospital logo on large sheets so he could see how it would all come together.

Once that was done, he constructed the mural at home, which included cutting the tiles and organizing them into sections. When the tiles for the mural were finished, they needed to be installed at the hospital. Tom Hilbert, a professional tile installer from the community, volunteered a lot of time teaching Thad how to grout and place the tiles on the wall. "He did the actual installing, and I helped him," Thad says. "We discovered along the way that he was also an Eagle Scout!"

Finally, the tiles needed to be washed off, which brought many people out to help. Countless people supported Thad and his project at its various stages, including his friends, church members, other Boy Scouts, and his family.

"I was inspired by my older sister who had done a lot of volunteering at the hospital," Thad says. "She put a lot of smiles on the children's faces, and I wanted to do that too."

During the years he worked on the project, Thad spent a day as a patient at the hospital, sick with pneumonia. His mom, Lynne Taylor, says this only affirmed what he was doing. "It gave him a good taste of what the kids who go in and out of the hospital go through, and gave him a little more satisfaction in knowing how his wall will help bring a little cheer to sick kids and their families."

The three years that Thad worked on the project weren't always easy. But Thad hopes his work can inspire others to help the people around them by volunteering. "A community is just a conglomeration of individuals, but everyone has to do their part in order to keep that community alive," Thad says. "Volunteering is about showing that you believe there is something bigger than just yourself. It's about displaying to others that you value them just as much as yourself. There are so many lessons you learn by volunteering, and those are lessons you're going to carry for the rest of your life."

Angela McKnight

"Carepreneur"

*A*ngela McKnight's work caring for seniors began with her own family. When her granny became ill, Angela helped as she could from a distance. Then her mother got sick, and Angela was able to provide care in her mother's own home. After her mother passed away, Angela's granny became ill again, and Angela brought her home to be with her. Angela's mission with both of these women she loved was to make sure they were well taken care of until they died.

Angela wanted to make sure other seniors were also able to age with dignity—knowing they had worth and deserved respect. She began Angela Cares and Care About You, two organizations in New Jersey that work to help seniors stay in their own homes as they get older. Their motto is "A passion to care. The ability to help."

They do help, in all kinds of ways. They get seniors signed up for Meals on Wheels, which brings food right to their homes. Food stamps can also aid seniors who are struggling with money, and the organizations help them fill out the applications. They encourage fitness, help with money matters, and make sure the people know about services that can make their lives better. They even help out with computers or housekeeping if there's a need! They spend time with these elders and keep them company. There are volunteers that can help with just about anything.

Angela has made many people feel loved, and made it possible for them to stay safely and joyfully in their own homes. "You are truly an angel," one senior named Ms. Lillie said. "Your name should have been Angel. Mr. James and I needed help, and God sent you here. Thank you for caring for seniors, because we are solemnly forgotten."

Angela and her organizations are also committed to helping other caregivers who are taking care of elderly friends or family. When you're a caregiver, it's easy to feel alone and without support. Angela remembers feeling lost and feeling that she had nowhere to turn as she cared for her mother and granny. She doesn't want others to feel this way. She encourages caregivers to ask for help, because having help from others is what makes it possible to keep caring. "Caring for your senior loved one or ones is priceless," she says.

Part of the commitment to caregivers includes educating and mentoring caregivers and youth who are taking care of seniors in their lives. Angela and her staff get to know each person they encounter so they can understand their needs and goals. "We show our clients that we care with compassion, integrity, and respect," she says.

As a large part of Angela's ministry, she wants to make sure seniors are eating in a nutritious way. Sometimes, knowing what to feed the person you are caring for can seem difficult. Caregivers get discouraged. Angela wrote a book called *Caregiver's Guide to Helping Seniors Eat Healthy*. This teaches simple, easy ways to make sure seniors are receiving the nutrition they need. Angela says it is never too late to learn to eat healthy!

Angela's passion to help others is one of her main interests. She wants to make her community a better place through her actions. She believes helping, mentoring, empowering, and supporting others will make a positive impact. This will make life better for people of every generation, from youth and their parents to the elders they serve.

Brad Hurtig

Motivational speaker

*I*t had to be the worst day of Brad's life," Keenan Culler says, "but there he was, worried about how everyone else was holding up."

Brad Hurtig, a seventeen-year-old from a small Ohio town, had just lost both of his hands in a work accident. He and Keenan, his best friend, miscommunicated, and a five-hundred-ton machine came down on Brad's arms. The pain was overwhelming. The future looked bleak. Brad was a three-sport athlete, and he knew the prospect of ever playing a game again was dim.

But Brad didn't give up. He also didn't want the accident to ruin anyone else's life. "This is not your fault," he told his boss. "Tell Keenan it's not his either."

Brad spent the summer recovering, and by fall was ready to get back on the field. The trainers wrapped specially designed pads around the ends of his arms, and he went to practice. It wasn't easy. It took a lot of energy just *watching* his teammates. One day Brad needed a drink of water. He saw a water bottle lying at his coach's feet and asked for a drink. Brad's coach glanced at the water bottle, then at Brad, then back at the water bottle. Instead of reaching for it, his coach looked Brad in the eye and said something he'll never forget: "If you're thirsty enough, you'll find a way."

"Find a way." This became Brad's motto. His coach's words reminded him that he had a choice about what his life would look like.

"After the accident I wasn't able to do very much for myself," Brad says. "I depended on people around me. Thankfully, my family helped with all of my basic needs—showering, brushing my teeth, getting dressed. The fact that I could depend on them meant I wasn't alone, and that took away a lot of my fear." Brad's brother even carried his lunch tray and spoonfed him at school! Working together, they found a way.

By his senior year, Brad earned back the starting middle linebacker position. He led his team with 111 tackles and was honored as a first team all-state linebacker.

"He chose not to despair," his friend Carol Kurivial says. "I am always amazed by his beautiful spirit, his beautiful generosity, his compassion." Seeing this, Carol suggested that Brad do some public speaking, but he wasn't ready.

"I remember telling God, 'I'm never going to be in front of people,'" he says. "That will never be my calling. I can't do that."

But it turns out, it *was* his calling. "He's changing a lot of people's lives because of the story he tells," Keenan says.

"We all have challenges in life," Brad says. "We all have setbacks. How we handle those setbacks will in many ways define our lives. The ability to deal with adversity, the ability to find a way when it doesn't seem like there is a way, will set us apart from others. You won't listen to how others put you down or to that voice that says you're not good enough."

Brad wants others to thrive no matter what happens in their lives. That's why he's devoted himself to speaking at schools, with youth groups, and being involved with the Fellowship of Christian Athletes. "There might be times you find yourself in the same place," he says. "What are you going to do?" He smiles. "If you're thirsty enough, you'll find a way."

Evie Webb

Dog treat maker

$\mathcal{E}$vie Webb was three years old in 2010 when an earthquake hit Haiti. The earthquake had a magnitude of 7.3 and killed 230,000 people. "In 2015 my dad told me how some people in Haiti live in really small houses, because their houses got destroyed, or were living in tents in tent communities," Evie says. "He showed me how big the houses in Haiti were by comparing them to our downstairs bathroom. Some houses were about the same size, or just a little bigger. I was shocked at this realization. Then he told me that many people still didn't have homes since the earthquake."

Evie wanted to do something to help build houses in Haiti. She had just finished traveling around the United States with her family on a their "one year road trip." Over fourteen months they visited every state and met with youth who are making the world a better place through "changemaker" projects. "I wanted to be a changemaker too," Evie says. But she wasn't sure how to start. "My dad asked me three questions: What do I love? What am I good at? And what do I know? I love dogs, I'm pretty good at baking, and I knew that many families in Haiti were still living in tents."

So Evie started Evie's Dog Treats. For a donation, Evie would bake homemade dog biscuits. She decided to make them out of whole wheat flour, peanut butter, baking powder, oats, and milk. Dogs loved them, and they were tasty enough that people could eat them too! She cut them into fun holiday shapes and shapes that went with the season.

Evie set a goal of $3,000, the amount needed to purchase a home for a family in Haiti through an organization called the Maxima Foundation. Maxima would buy the building supplies and build the house right there where the family would live.

Evie started an online account so people could place an order and donate money, but she also went to a lot of dog parks. She would sit outside the gate and sell the treats. "Sometimes we brought our skates, and we would skate around, asking people if they wanted some," she says. Evie also rented a booth at the local farmers' market, where she sold ornaments, homemade dog toys, and other items to help boost donations.

Evie's project took a lot of work, but in two years she was able to raise the money she needed. The Maxima Foundation even matched her donation! This meant she was able to build two houses instead of just one. And after the houses were built, Evie had a chance to travel to Haiti with her family to see the houses and meet the families.

Even though the project was Evie's responsibility, her family helped a lot too. Her parents helped her to understand the situation in Haiti and figure out how she could help. Evie says her family, friends, and church helped out, encouraged her, and supported her.

Evie's first project with Evie's Dog Treats moved steadily, and she was able to help two families get new homes. She is still happy to make dog treats for people who like them and want to support the project, although this time she is raising money more slowly, since she is busy with school and other activities. Sometimes peacemaking happens quickly, and sometimes it moves along at a slow, steady pace. Either way, the work gets done!

Pastor Ignacio Chamorro Ramírez

Prison pastor

*P*astor Ignacio Chamorro Ramírez wasn't always a pastor. In fact, he didn't always go to church. He grew up on the streets in Paraguay, and he made some pretty bad choices. When he was nineteen, he was arrested for robbery. He spent twenty days in jail.

"It was a traumatic experience, but made no change in my life," he says. When he got out of jail he continued with his life of crime.

A few years later he was arrested and sent to prison for a crime he didn't commit. He was not charged for the ones he actually did! He was sent to the Tacumbu prison, which is the largest, most violent prison in Paraguay. It was built many years ago, and made to hold eight hundred prisoners. Now there are almost four thousand people imprisoned there! This makes it very hard for the prison guards to control what happens between the inmates, and there is much fighting and violence. It also means there's not enough room for people to be taken care of or have any privacy. Ignacio grew angry and bitter while he was in prison at Tacumbu, and if anyone ever invited him to church, he said no.

One day a friend of his in the prison was going to study math. Ignacio decided to go with him. "The person leading talked about God, but I had nothing else to do, so I stayed," he says. "There, God touched my heart. Something new began in my life."

This math instructor introduced Ignacio to La Libertad, a church that serves men inside the prison. La Libertad means "freedom" in English. The La Libertad congregation is a ministry of the Concordia Mennonite Brethren Church. They began this prison ministry all the way back in 1984. The Paraguayan government's Ministry of Justice agreed to let the church work with one block of the prison's inmates—about 535 men. The church's focus is to teach the men about God, themselves, and prayer. It also educates them about other things to round out their knowledge. They work on literacy—reading and writing— and skills that will help the prisoners get jobs when they're released. One hundred and thirty inmates participate in the church.

After his first meeting with the math instructor, Ignacio started to get involved with La Libertad. "I learned about the benefit of discipleship . . . was baptized, and began to do for others what they had done for me."

After Ignacio got out of prison, he went back to school to get his high school diploma. Once he was done with that, he studied theology—God, faith, and the church—at Instituto Bíblico Asunción. He also began working with La Libertad. He has been with them since 2012. Ignacio believes in the forgiveness of sins. The members of the church have done many bad things, causing harm to themselves and others. Ignacio believes they can all be forgiven and changed through the death and resurrection of Jesus.

Pastor Ignacio feels strongly that having a church within the prison is important. "It provides opportunity to recover dignity, economic freedom, and most important, to grow and develop the person's life in Christ, and to continue to journey in love," he says. "God has power. God changes people."

Anna Groff

Abuse prevention advocate

*C*hild abuse, when an adult causes harm to a child or youth, is something people don't like to talk about. Anna Groff believes we *need* to talk about it. In her work with young people she has seen firsthand how important it is for children to learn about safety, caring for their bodies, and healthy relationships. The more children know and understand, the better able they are to have healthy relationships and to speak out when they are being harmed.

Anna knows that things aren't always easy for young people. Kids and youth have a lot of challenges as they figure out friendships, technology, social media, and everyday school stresses. "I truly believe God cares about all this," Anna says. "God loves you and wants you to be safe, loved, and cared for." Anna also wants churches to take the health and safety of young people seriously, and she wants children and youth to know that the church is a place where no topic is off-limits. Anna says, "Church should be a place for you to ask questions about things that worry you or scare you. We don't have to put on a smile and pretend it is all okay. God cares about your body and soul and mind and heart."

And Jesus does too! When Anna thinks about young people, she tries to imagine them through the eyes of Jesus. She says, "When the disciples ask Jesus who ranks high in God's kingdom, Jesus doesn't say we're all equal. Jesus actually brings a child into the conversation." The status of children in Bible times was not much better than that of someone who was a slave. But Jesus tells the disciples to become like children. Jesus understood that children are important and have important ideas to share—ideas that adults might never have even thought of.

Because Anna cares so much about young people, she works hard to protect them from harm. Anna helps churches to have conversations about what it means to care for one another in all ways—body, mind, and spirit. She also helps them to create plans to keep young people safe and to find ways to talk openly if something bad does happen, so that everyone can feel safe moving forward.

Anna knows that all of us, and especially children, learn about God's love through our relationships with others. That's why it's so important that adults take responsibility for protecting children and believe them when they say they've been hurt. "God looks out for God's sheep—us," Anna says. "And adults are called to do the same for the children in our communities."

One way that Anna helps children and youth is through a special curriculum called *Circle of Grace*. The curriculum invites children to see themselves with an imaginary circle around them, a circle of grace. They are empowered to invite whom and what they want into their circle, and to get help from a trusted adult if someone or something enters their circle that is unwanted or harmful. Anna says that people of all ages need help understanding and respecting boundaries.

The work that Anna does is important, and it is work that she loves. She believes that churches that want to live the love of Jesus need to teach children that God loves their whole selves; they need to respect children's boundaries; and they must defend and protect them always.

Brock Miller

Prayer walker

In 2014, two young men in Lancaster, Pennsylvania, broke into the home of a young schoolteacher named Nicole Mathewson. They wanted to steal money, or whatever they could find that had any value. Nicole got in their way, and they killed her.

The people in Nicole's neighborhood and surrounding streets were sad, frightened, and angry. How could something like this happen? Why did these two men bring violence to their town? Nicole was an innocent bystander. People began to realize that this tragedy could have happened to any of them. Suddenly, even though not everyone knew Nicole, the situation felt personal, and they were angry and afraid.

Brock Miller and a few of his friends wanted to do something. They *needed* to do something. But what? What could possibly make a difference and help stop the violence in their neighborhood? What kinds of actions would help people want to live peacefully? When people are angry and scared, they react in different ways. Some fight back with violence. Some protest. Some keep to themselves, peeking out from behind their closed doors. Some argue with each other about the right way to respond.

Brock and his friends decided that instead of reacting to Nicole's death with their own anger and violence, they would do two things: walk and pray. Every morning they met on the sidewalk in front of Nicole's house to remember her and think about their neighborhood's pain, anger, and loss. They prayed over the houses, the people, and each other. They walked up and down the streets, praying for everyone they saw, carrying lit candles as symbols of light in the darkness. They stopped in the park to pray for the children who played there. They walked to the schools and prayed for the students. They blessed streets and businesses. They even went to the nearby prison to pray for the inmates.

For the first few weeks new people showed up every day. They met and got to know each other by praying and walking together. They chose to do this instead of hiding in their houses, armed with guns. They wanted to show that they really did want peace, and wanted to work toward it in a peaceable way.

All kinds of people came to walk and pray. There was a college student, home for Christmas break, who drove up from another town. A mom whose daughter lived in the neighborhood. Someone who was a close friend of Nicole. Parents with young children, and pastors, and employees of local businesses. People from different places, with different life experiences and different abilities, all joined together to work toward a more peaceful town.

After the first month, not everyone could come anymore. Soon it was just Brock and his friends, the ones who started the prayer walk. They meet once a week to walk the streets and pray for their neighbors. They believe peaceful activism is something Jesus himself would do. He would act locally and do something that involved the community. Sometimes activism is big and loud and angry, but it can also be small and quiet and prayerful.

Nicole Mathewson's death sparked peace in Lancaster. Brock Miller's prayer is that everyone will feel the blessing he and his friends lay on the sidewalks as their feet walk the streets.

Emily Teng

Chief of Awesome

*E*mily Teng loves the word *awesome*. Besides being her favorite word, it's also how she sees the world and her role in it. Every day she wants to go out and help young people find their own "inner awesomeness" and see how they can change the world. That's why she started a project called Beyond Awesome.

She, the founder, uses the title "Chief of Awesome."

As a young girl, Emily moved around a lot. She got the idea for Beyond Awesome because of some of her experiences growing up in different places—Jakarta, Melbourne, and Singapore. She was very shy in school, and was bullied for several years. She says, "I was constantly taunted, teased, and told how ugly I was, how I would never amount to anything, how dumb I was, how stupid I sounded when I asked questions in class that I didn't understand—the list goes on."

Emily was able to overcome these problems and her shyness. She even ended up working as a DJ on a radio station for several years! She believes God gave her the strength to change. Through prayer she learned to depend on God and trust that God would guide her one step at a time. And since God helped her, she wanted to help others.

Beyond Awesome is a program in Singapore for children and youth ages six through sixteen. It's a safe space where children can have access to opportunities that they might not have otherwise. Children come to Beyond Awesome for free education. There's a focus on reading and making sure the students get the educational resources they need, because academics are very important in Singapore, and students feel pressure to do well.

One special experience in the school is called Jalan Jalan. On these field trips the students visit a workplace or a place of special interest in the city. This connects them to adults who can be role models and mentors. It helps the students see things in a way they hadn't before. Emily wants the children to discover what is possible for them, rather than what is not.

Emily believes studies are important, but more than that, she wants students to learn about kindness, confidence, and compassion. They learn these things by making new friends and having deep, meaningful conversations with volunteers. The volunteers want the children to learn that the community is there to lift each other up. They want the students to grow to be people who help others and serve in their communities.

Many of the volunteers at Beyond Awesome are young people. The youth volunteers come in to serve and learn right alongside the kids! They find meaning and connection in these relationships. Beyond Awesome is a place to belong and develop a sense of worth and value through helping younger children.

"If you experience love yourself," Emily says, "you will then share with other people. I want love not to be a cheesy cliché thing, but I want love to be seen as a superpower and something that people will catch on and spread with joy in this city. We are so connected through technology and social media, but really are so disconnected. This group wants to connect on a human, personal level."

Beyond Awesome does just that.

"Go into the world and do well," their website says. "But more importantly, go into the world and do good."

Pastor Gavin Rogers

Pastor for all people

Gavin Rogers is a pastor at Travis Park United Methodist Church in San Antonio, Texas. A lot of his work is with people who are poor and homeless in his city. Sometimes his ministry takes unexpected paths, and he learns about people in unusual ways.

In November 2018, he traveled with a group of immigrants—known in the United States as the "caravan"—as they made their way toward the southern U.S. border.

After hearing so much in the news about these people, he wanted to find out what was really going on. He flew to Mexico City and asked where he could find the caravan. No one was exactly sure, so he put on his backpack and started walking. He found a group of young people from Honduras and Guatemala who welcomed him into their group. They were young, because only young people were able to make the long journey. He traveled with them for five days. As they walked, he took pictures and filmed interviews and used his phone to share them on social media.

The young people treated Pastor Gavin with love and care. "They did as the Scriptures ask," he says. "They treated me as a stranger in a foreign land. They embraced me. They had every right to greet me, then say they needed to get moving. Instead, they made sure I was safe, gave me food and water, and treated me as family. When we were traveling on the top of an eighteen-wheeler, they tied me down to make sure I wouldn't fall. I became one of the travelers."

The group traveled in large numbers because that was safer than traveling alone. They could care for each other and keep their families together. They moved from camp to camp, where they would charge their phones and get in touch with their families back home. They carried clothing, blankets, and what little money they had on their backs.

Pastor Gavin had heard people in the United States say the immigrants were criminals. He found no evidence that the immigrants were doing anything wrong. They were running *away* from criminals. They simply wanted a better life. Some Americans thought they were coming to the United States to take what the Americans believed was theirs—jobs, homes, money. But the people on the journey didn't want that. They just wanted a safe place to live. They wanted a way to support their family. They wanted their children to go to school.

After Pastor Gavin returned to San Antonio, the travelers arrived in Tijuana, Mexico. They applied to enter the United States as refugees and were told to . . . wait. The waiting was going to be very long, and the camp where they were expected to stay was awful. The tents didn't keep out rain, and the bathroom facilities were unsanitary. Pastor Gavin connected his friends with a local priest in Mexico, who found a place for them to stay.

Pastor Gavin was surprised at some of the questions he heard from people in the United States. They asked him, "So if one of them stole your coat, you would just say it was okay?" Pastor Gavin was astounded. Jesus had to answer that exact question! "I could copy and paste your question and it would pop up in the Bible," he told them. "His answer is to let them keep the coat."

"We forget that Jesus was a migrant," Pastor Gavin says. "As people of faith, we have to remember that. We have to treat today's immigrants with the love and generosity we would give him."

Alyssa Deraco

Book lover

*A*lyssa Deraco has always loved reading. When she was ten years old, she began looking for a way to help children who might not have the same opportunities that she did, and wondered how she could do that with books. "I picked books because they helped me through my parents' divorce," she says. "I enjoy helping others, and I wanted to give kids who don't have much of a way to forget their troubles by reading. Books have helped me, and I want to share my love of books and reading with kids to help them too."

It was during this time she needed a project for her Girl Scout Bronze Award. It seemed the perfect time to start giving. Alyssa collected books to give to children at Milagro House, a local homeless shelter. When the project was over, she wanted to keep helping. She started a nonprofit called Alyssa's Bedtime Stories and expanded her ministry. She wants to make sure that children have something to open at the holidays. The organization gives away between five hundred and nine hundred packages each year containing several books, a pair of pajamas, and a toothbrush.

"We are dedicated to giving hope to children through a simple act of kindness and generosity," Alyssa says. Since 2009, Alyssa's Bedtime Stories has donated over ten thousand books and five thousand pairs of pajamas to children who are homeless, have experienced abuse at home, or simply can't afford to buy books for themselves.

Alyssa's mother was a huge part of getting the charity started. As the organization grew, the two of them soon realized that they needed more help. Several of Alyssa's friends joined in. "Whenever they have an event, they run it," Alyssa's mom says. The volunteers take on a lot of responsibility.

Every time Alyssa's Bedtime Stories gives a package to someone in their local area, it is personalized, labeled by name, and hand-delivered. "We got to go and hand the children their presents," says Korynn, one of Alyssa's friends. "We got to eat with them, and it was really, really fun." The volunteers enjoy getting to know the children and developing relationships. They share in the joy of the gifts together.

Alyssa loves helping others, but also sees that giving of herself changes her own life too. "I do get something from it," Alyssa says. "I get to see how happy they are, and I get to know that I'm making a difference in the world."

Alyssa's relationship with her mother has also grown as they work together. One afternoon, Alyssa says, "we were arguing, and it was bad. We had to drop off a donation. So we went to Milagro House, and we saw the kids and everything. Right after that we were fine and happy and hugged each other."

"We were arguing about something so dumb," Alyssa's mom says. "It kind of brings you back to reality."

Alyssa wants to see the charity expand. She has sent packages to Panama and Ecuador, and hopes to be able to travel there someday to give the books personally. She also traveled to Boston with Lancaster County Bible Church, and took books to give away as part of her team's ministry.

Alyssa wants to see books in the hands of every kid. "Books open the doors of our imagination," she says. "For children without a home, reading is more than just a pastime, it's a window into a better world."

Michael "MJ" Sharp

Conflict resolver

*D*uring grade school and junior high, Michael Sharp, or MJ, was attracted to the first part of Ecclesiastes 9:10. He said it fit him.

"Whatever your hand finds to do, do it with all your might" (NIV).

MJ liked this Bible verse because it was how he lived. He did everything at one hundred percent until he was doing it the best he possibly could. He was good at learning new things. He would become an expert quickly, then move on to something else. It was the challenge that drew him to a project.

Peacemaking was one thing MJ did one hundred percent, and it came to him naturally. Students told his parents, John and Michele, that MJ noticed them on the fringes. He made a special effort to be friends with them. He had a soft heart, and he cared about how other kids were treated.

This didn't always work out well. In elementary school, MJ befriended a boy who was shy and included him in his own circle of friends. When the boy didn't get into the same classes as MJ, he became a bully and made MJ's life pretty miserable. But this didn't stop MJ from helping others. He continued wanting to be a peacemaker.

MJ went to college at Eastern Mennonite University, in Virginia. After he graduated, he lived in Germany, where he worked with the Military Counseling Network. This is a project of the Mennonite church in Germany. His job was to form friendships with U.S. servicemembers who were stationed in Germany. MJ especially helped people who had life-changing experiences on the battlefield. They wanted to become conscientious objectors, which means they didn't want to fight anymore. MJ learned a lot about the lives of these soldiers. He also learned a lot about weapons, guns, and ammunition.

After serving there for three years, MJ went back to school, this time in Germany. He earned a master's degree in peace studies and conflict resolution. Conflict resolution means helping people work out problems peacefully.

In 2012, MJ used his education and experience to travel to the Democratic Republic of the Congo, a country in Africa. There he served with Mennonite Central Committee. He and his friends tried to get rebel groups to stop fighting. These groups also forced children to be soldiers, and MJ worked to return the children and their families to their homes.

A few years later MJ was hired by the United Nations, which is a group of countries that work to keep peace around the world. He worked as an expert on militia groups in Congo to try to stop the violence. He knew this was not a "safe" job, but felt called to it. In 2017, MJ and his coworker Zaida Catalán were killed by some people who were threatened by their work.

MJ's parents want to keep his peacemaking work going. "MJ told us, 'If something happened to me in Congo . . . maybe the United States and the world would pay attention,'" his dad says. "'All these years, nobody seems to care about what is going on in Congo. But if a white guy like me gets killed or something happens, maybe the people would pay attention.' It's exactly what happened. Exactly."

MJ's friends and family set up a scholarship at Eastern Mennonite University for graduate students to study at the school's Center for Justice and Peacebuilding. In this way, MJ is still doing his part—one hundred percent—to make the world a more peaceful place.

Bible Verses about Working for Peace

Whoever has two shirts must share with the one who has none, and whoever has food must do the same. **—LUKE 3:11**

Oh, let me sing about faithful love and justice! I want to sing my praises to you, Lord! **—PSALM 101:1**

Then those who are righteous will reply to him, "Lord, when did we see you hungry and feed you, or thirsty and give you a drink? When did we see you as a stranger and welcome you, or naked and give you clothes to wear? When did we see you sick or in prison and visit you?"

Then the king will reply to them, "I assure you that when you have done it for one of the least of these brothers and sisters of mine, you have done it for me." **—MATTHEW 25:37-40**

Jesus reached for a little child, placed him among the Twelve, and embraced him. Then he said, "Whoever welcomes one of these children in my name welcomes me; and whoever welcomes me isn't actually welcoming me but rather the one who sent me." **—MARK 9:36-37**

Happy are people who make peace, because they will be called God's children. —**MATTHEW 5:9**

The Lord has filled him with the divine spirit that will give him skill, ability, and knowledge for every kind of work. He will be able to create designs, do metalwork in gold, silver, and copper, cut stones for setting, carve wood, do every kind of creative work. —**EXODUS 35:31-33**

Don't pay back anyone for their evil actions with evil actions, but show respect for what everyone else believes is good. If possible, to the best of your ability, live at peace with all people. —**ROMANS 12:17-18**

So then, with endurance, let's also run the race that is laid out in front of us, since we have such a great cloud of witnesses surrounding us. Let's throw off any extra baggage, get rid of the sin that trips us up, and fix our eyes on Jesus.
—**HEBREWS 12:1-2**

[The LORD] said to me, "My grace is enough for you, because power is made perfect in weakness." So I'll gladly spend my time bragging about my weaknesses so that Christ's power can rest on me. Therefore, I'm all right with weaknesses, insults, disasters, harassments, and stressful situations for the sake of Christ, because when I'm weak, then I'm strong.
—**2 CORINTHIANS 12:9-10**

Then God said, "Let us make humanity in our image to resemble us so that they may take charge of the fish of the sea, the birds in the sky, the livestock, all the earth, and all the crawling things on earth." —**GENESIS 1:26**

Don't withhold good from someone who deserves it, when it is in your power to do so. Don't say to your neighbor, "Go and come back; I'll give it to you tomorrow," when you have it. Don't plan to harm your neighbor who trusts and lives near you.
—**PROVERBS 3:27-29**

God will judge between the nations, and settle disputes of mighty nations. Then they will beat their swords into iron plows and their spears into pruning tools. Nation will not take up sword against nation; they will no longer learn how to make war. —**ISAIAH 2:4**

When immigrants live in your land with you, you must not cheat them. Any immigrant who lives with you must be treated as if they were one of your citizens. You must love them as yourself, because you were immigrants in the land of Egypt; I am the Lord your God. —**LEVITICUS 19:33-34**

Speak out on behalf of the voiceless, and for the rights of all who are vulnerable. Speak out in order to judge with righteousness and to defend the needy and the poor.
—**PROVERBS 31:8-9**

Learn to do good. Seek justice: help the oppressed; defend the orphan; plead for the widow. —**ISAIAH 1:17**

Love the Lord your God with all your heart, with all your being, with all your mind, and with all your strength. . . . Love your neighbor as yourself. No other commandment is greater than these. —**MARK 12:30-31**

The Author

JUDY CLEMENS wrote the Agatha- and Anthony-nominated Stella Crown series, the Grim Reaper mysteries, and the stand-alone *Lost Sons* (published by Herald Press). Her YA thriller *Tag, You're Dead*, written as J.C. Lane, was also nominated for the Agatha and Anthony awards. She is a past-president of Sisters in Crime, a reviewer for the New York Journal of Books, and the mother of two young adults, which helps when writing YA and middle-grade fiction.

The Illustrator

DAVID LEONARD began his freelance illustration career in the first grade, trading colorings for pencils. He has never stopped drawing. His goal has never been to put an image on paper, but to capture a moment in time with gestures, emotions and paint strokes while reflecting his own fun, humorous, and whimsical personality. Telling stories through illustration on everything from books to billboards, David has worked with clients such as Amazon, Major League Baseball, Dr. Pepper, Random House, Warner Music, *Highlights for Children*, *The New Yorker*, and Shine curriculum (published by MennoMedia). When David is not illustrating, he enjoys feeding his snails and flying with his loving, forgiving, understanding, and supportive wife and their little, art-directing twin daughters.